HOW TO
QUIT YOUR JOB,
LIVE YOUR DREAMS,
AND MAKE SIX FIGURES YOUR
FIRST YEAR FLIPPING REAL ESTATE

FLIP YOUR FUTURE

RYAN PINEDA

Dedication

To my wonderful wife, Mindy, who has supported me and continues to stand by me in this journey. None of this would be possible without your faith. Thank you for your endless belief in me and for encouraging me to pursue my dreams.

To my incredible family, which has helped mold me into who I am today. I'm forever grateful for your unconditional love and support. Thank you for giving me all the tools to succeed.

To my awesome friends, who I also consider part of my family. Having such genuine relationships has been a blessing. Thank you for being there and keeping me humble.

Lastly to all my coaches and mentors, who have pushed me to new levels. Thank you for all the hours you've put into training, inspiring, and guiding me.

"For I know the plans I have for you," declares the Lord, "plans to prosper you and not to harm you, plans to give you hope and a future."

Jeremiah 29:11

CONTENTS

Introduction

Dreams. They are what push us forward and give us hope for the future. I'm guessing you have always thought that there was something greater in store for you. As the years have gone on, maybe your dreams have started to fade away. You might be stuck in a job that you hate or in a career that's stalled out. Perhaps you got your degree and found out that you were lied to. You were told employers would be lining up to hire you for your dream job. That hasn't happened. Now you have student loan debt and don't know what the next step is. It feels like your dreams couldn't be further away, and the future you envisioned suddenly looks a lot less likely.

If you're reading this book, then you have decided that you may want to *Flip Your Future*. You may not have any idea how it's going to happen, but you're open to trying anything. Your dream might be to travel the world. Perhaps it's to own a home on the beach. Maybe you want to be able to spend more time with your family.

You may not even know what your dreams are anymore. The dreams you had growing up might no longer be possible. That's okay! When one dream closes, it opens up a door for a new one to begin. I know this was the case for me. I was very blessed to reach my dream early on in life. But once it ended, I didn't know what I wanted anymore.

Thankfully, I was introduced to real estate. I now firmly believe that investing in real estate can lead you to your dreams. It provided me a solution when I didn't know what I wanted to do. Now it's allowed me to have the freedom to do what I want and make a lot of money along the way. How did I get to this point?

CHAPTER 1:

My Journey

Growing up, I had no plans to pursue a career in real estate. I always wanted to be a professional baseball player. I'm not sure I've ever met anyone who wanted to be a real estate investor growing up. People from all walks of life end up in the industry somehow. Part of the reason I fell into it was because of my mom. She has been a real estate agent since before I was alive! I don't know what made her want to do it, but I know it provided our family with a great life growing up. We were always able to go on family vacations, baseball tournaments, and anything we wanted to do. So many of my friend's parents couldn't come to baseball games or events because they were held down by their "normal" jobs. I noticed we never had those types of problems with my mom being in real estate and my dad being self-employed.

Fast forward to 2010. I'm 21 years old and I had just completed my college baseball career at Cal State Northridge. I had been a Freshman All American, Freshman Conference Player of the Year, and an All Conference selection among other things. On Draft Day I was fortunate enough to hear my name called by the Oakland A's. Finally, all my hard work had paid off and my dreams had come true. I signed my contract and began my professional career.

I will never forget that experience. Our team was in Vancouver, Canada and we got to play in front of 5,000 fans every single night. I was living my dream! But there is a funny thing about minor league baseball that a lot of people don't know: You don't get paid anything close to what the big leaguers get! Our salary was $1,200 a month. When you factor in how many hours we were at the field, weight room, and road trips, it's actually less than minimum wage. To make matters worse, you only get paid in the season, which is about five months long. So my annual income was about $6,000. As you can see, that's not much to live on. As a result, most guys have to get an off-season job. So this was the beginning of my career in real estate.

I knew I needed something that would allow me to have my own schedule. A normal job wasn't going to let me leave for five months every year. I also needed the freedom to train and practice so I could work towards getting to the big leagues. So I took a play from my mom and decided to become a real estate agent. I finished real estate school a month later and passed the test. There was one problem, though. It was 2010 in Las Vegas, Nevada.

We were still in a recession and Vegas was hit harder than any other city in the United States. So it was extremely hard to find clients! To make matters worse, the commissions weren't much when I did close deals! I made about $20,000 that first year as an agent. I had no idea what I was doing and looking back at it now, I was very fortunate to have made that much.

Being an agent taught me a lot of things, though. It helped me learn how to write contracts, negotiate with other agents, and search the MLS (Multiple Listing Service) for deals. In 2011, my cousin and I decided we wanted to buy a house together. After months of searching, we settled on a nice four-bedroom home for $160,000. That same home had sold for $400,000 just a couple of years earlier!

If I'm being honest, it wasn't even a good deal. It was where we wanted to live and it fit our needs so we bought it. We also rented out the other two rooms to our buddies. That house quickly turned into a mess with the four of us, but it was a blast!

After about two years there, we decided it was time to sell and cash out. We both didn't have a lot of money so it was the logical thing to do. During those two years the market appreciated and we were able to sell it for $215,000. I didn't know it at the time, but that would be the first of many flips. If the market had not appreciated, I wouldn't have been able to make a profit. So my first flip ended up being a success because of pure luck!

After that first flip, I had a little bit of money and I decided to buy another property. This time it was a good deal, so I had equity built in from the start. I was also about to leave for another baseball season so I rented it out.

A couple things happened after that. As the season went on, I started to run low on money. I was engaged to my fiancée, Mindy, and we had a wedding we needed to pay for. So I thought to myself that it would be a good idea to sell the home. I told the tenant what that I was selling it and a funny thing happened. They wanted to buy the house! So we agreed on a price and they ended up buying it. I owned the property for six months and made a $26,000 profit on it.

Later that year, Mindy and I got married. We had spent most of the profit on the wedding and a new car. Because of that, we had to live in an apartment. We believed that God would provide another home for us if we were patient. Almost six months later, He did and we moved into our first real home together.

Pretty soon after buying it, I began to think about flipping it. I started running the numbers and seeing the dollar signs! This time it was different, though, because I had a wife! She said we weren't moving and I was not about to challenge her on that. No amount of money is worth an angry wife!

So, I thought my flipping days were over unless one of my friends or family gave me a pile of money to invest. Unfortunately for me, I didn't know anyone like that. My parents were crushed by the recession and all my friends were strapped with college debt. There was no angel investor in sight.

So I had a decision to make on how I wanted to provide for my family. Mindy was in school and wasn't working. I had been a real estate agent for four years at this point. I wasn't very good at it and I didn't have any clients. All the money we made from the flip was quickly dwindling. Things got so bad that I stopped doing real estate and started flipping furniture on Craigslist! I sold my brand new car and bought a 10-year-old truck just so I could flip couches and pay the bills.

Flipping furniture was definitely not my dream! I for sure didn't want it to be my future! I was at a crossroads in my life, and I had no idea what to do. So I got on my knees and prayed that God would show me a different way. I knew I was meant for more, but I had no idea what.

CHAPTER 2:

The Epiphany

Shortly after that prayer, my wife and I went to New Orleans to celebrate our first anniversary. We were going to watch the Packers (my favorite team) play the Saints. I had put flipping houses on the back burner and not given it much thought.

Our first night in the hotel I was scrolling through the TV channels and I found one of those house-flipping shows. We started watching, and during the commercial break they had an advertisement about their upcoming seminar. They claimed you could flip houses with no money down! Naturally, I was skeptical so I ignored it and sat through the commercials. While I sat there, I had this idea to Google the seminar and see if it was a scam. So I pulled out my phone and typed "_____ seminar scam." (I'm not going to say whose seminar it was.)

The first pages that popped up were forum posts. In the posts the people talked about how they paid all this money and the program sucked. One said, "You can find all their information online for free." Then he linked a couple articles and books to read. I downloaded the books and went to bed.

The next day we went shopping (meaning my wife went shopping). As she walked through stores, I had my Kindle out and started reading these new books. I can't properly explain what happened the next couple hours, but my mind literally felt like it was going to explode!

The answers I had been searching for were right there! I finally had figured out how I could flip a lot of houses right now! I finished the book that day and started listening to podcasts nonstop. That became the real estate education that I needed. I now had the basic tools to flip houses instead of couches. We finished our trip by watching the Packers lose, but it didn't matter, because I had already won.

When we got back to Las Vegas, we had $10,000 in our savings account. This wasn't enough to cover what I needed to buy a property. So I called all my credit cards and got them to raise my limits. I had $50,000 in credit and I cash-advanced them all to the max. I was at the point of no return. Now I just had to find a deal.

A couple of weeks later I ended up finding one. I purchased it with hard money (we'll learn about that later) and used about $45,000 to cover the down payment and rehab costs. A week after that I saw another deal pop up. I didn't have much cash left, but I said to myself, *I've come this far, I might as well go all in.* So I used the rest of the money I had left to buy the second property. I'm not going to lie, I was extremely nervous! Ironically, Mindy wasn't fazed. She could see how excited I was about it and she trusted my judgment. I don't give her enough credit for how much faith she put into me!

Fast forward a few months and a few mistakes. Both homes sold and we made about $40,000 profit! So in five months I watched us go from having $10,000 in the bank to $50,000. It was crazy to think how quickly we were able to increase our money to five times the amount.

We never would have been able to do it unless we took that leap of faith with the credit cards. Now I'm not saying you should go max out your credit cards. I'm also not saying go cash out your 401k. But I am saying that in order to do this, you will need to take a leap of faith. That leap of faith will be different for everyone. No one has ever changed their life by staying in their comfort zone. So get ready to get uncomfortable!

CHAPTER 3:

New Mindset

A lot has changed since I bought those two properties back in 2015. In the three years since then, I have bought over 100 properties in various states. That initial $10,000 has grown to over $1,000,000 and I'm constantly reinvesting it into more deals. I've been blessed far beyond what I ever imagined just a short time ago. I now feel it's my duty to share my journey and teach others how to do the same. Even with over 100 purchases, I know I'm not nearly as experienced as others who have written books. But I know the system I've developed works, and it can make you six figures your first year doing it. So let's get into the *Flip Your Future System*.

Before you do anything else, you must first change your mindset. You need to be mentally prepared for the journey you're about to go on. There are a few things you must be willing to do in order to change your mindset.

1. *Eliminate Your False Beliefs.*

   "I need more money." This was my biggest false belief that prevented me from starting. In reality, I had all the money I needed. You might be thinking to yourself, *Ryan, I barely had enough money to buy this book!* Even if that's the case, eliminate that belief! There are multiple ways to invest with no money out of your pocket. In fact, most of the deals I do today I don't use my own money on. I'm going to teach you how I do it in the following chapters.

Money is actually the easiest part of flipping homes. There is more money out there than there are deals. So if money is the only thing holding you back, then get rid of that false belief.

"I don't have the time." We all have the same 24 hours every day. It's just a matter of whether you're willing to prioritize flipping houses above other things. Do you watch TV? Spend time browsing on social media? Go out on the weekends? If you do any of those things, then you have time. Starting out in this system, I need you to dedicate at least two hours a day to working on your house-flipping business. You don't need to quit your job yet; all you need is two hours a day. Eventually as your business grows, you'll be able to quit your job and have a lot more time! But it's going to take hard work to get to that point.

I started flipping houses while playing baseball in another state. So I know it's possible to do it even if you're not physically there! If you truly don't have the time because your life is that busy, then get a partner. Find someone who has time and learn this system together. I would rather you team up with someone so you both can live out your dreams together!

"I don't know how to fix things." Neither do I! I actually don't want to learn how to fix things because I don't want to do that stuff. I might be one of the most unhandy (is that even a word?) people in the world! So that shouldn't hold you back. I've figured out how to buy over 100 homes and I still haven't picked up a hammer. So this should not be a false belief for you. And none of these false beliefs should prevent you from starting.

2. *Network*

Networking is the number one thing that has made me successful. Up until 2016, I rarely posted on social media. I didn't want people to know my business or what I was up to. I also didn't want to be that "annoying person on Facebook." We all know this guy. They're the one who posts everyday about how awesome they are. Nobody likes that person.

So I stayed away from posting about my successes for a long time. Then one day my mentor convinced me to start doing it. So I listened to his advice and it has helped grow my business more than anything else. But in order for it to work, you need to be able to use it properly. We'll go over that later in the book. For now, just commit to being active on social media. You also need to commit to going to networking events. This includes lunches, coffee meetings, and real estate group meetings. Who wouldn't want to go have coffee and call it work?

3. *Take Risks*

There will be risk with every deal regardless of how good it looks. I've had plenty of deals that I thought were home runs and they turned out to be singles. You must be willing to accept that you might lose money on a deal. As of this writing, I've only lost money on one deal out of the 100+ I've purchased. I'll take those odds any day of the week! So I know the *Flip Your Future System* will teach you to safely invest. I just want you to be mentally prepared for the risks because nothing is guaranteed.

When I maxed out all my credit cards, I was confident I was buying a good deal. But I knew that if I was wrong, I could lose money. You have to be willing to accept that, because most people play scared. They don't want to risk anything. Someone said, "Scared money doesn't make money," and that couldn't be any truer. Change your mindset and have faith that it's going to work out!

CHAPTER 4:

Choosing a Market

Now that you're ready to start flipping homes, you need to choose your market. You will be looking for the following criteria in the market you choose.

1. **Population.** Ideally, you want to be flipping in markets with populations over 500,000. You can have success in markets with smaller populations, but it's a lot harder. You should not be in a market with fewer than 100,000 people. If your current market is smaller than that, then you need to find a new market. When you have a higher population, that means there are more homes. When you have more homes, it gives you a greater chance to find more deals. Small markets are tough because there aren't as many homes to choose from. Furthermore, when you go to sell, you won't have as many buyers looking for homes. This is not a good combination for flipping. If possible, try to be in markets with at least 500,000 people! If you're not able to be in those markets, then try to be in a market with a minimum of 100,000 people.

2. **DOM (Days on Market).** You must be aware of the average DOM in the market you choose to flip in. A local real estate agent can give you this information. A lower DOM is better because your home will sell faster. When your home sells faster, there are fewer costs and you can reinvest your money more frequently. The ideal DOM is less than 90

days. If it's more, I wouldn't advise investing in that market. If you want to flip in a market with a higher DOM, make sure you plan for extra holding costs.

3. **Inventory Levels.** To calculate inventory levels, take the active inventory and divide it by the amount of homes sold in the last 30 days. For example:

    Active Homes: 6324

    Homes Sold in the Last 30 Days: 3,250

    6,324/3,250 = **1.95 Months of Inventory**

    If there were no new homes to hit the market, the current active listings would sell in 1.95 months.

    One to three months of inventory is ideal. That means it's a seller's market. Buyers don't have a lot of options, so your home should sell fast. You can be aggressive with pricing your home higher and potentially making more profit.

    Four to five months of inventory is a neutral market. You don't have the advantage as a seller, because a buyer has more options now. You can still flip in this market, but plan on the property taking longer to sell. You could potentially price your flip cheaper to try to get a faster sell.

    Six months or more is a buyer's market. You will want to stay away from this market. Buyers control the game, and you may have to hold a property for a long time.

4. **Proximity.** You should look to flip in markets as close as possible to you. Flipping homes in your local area will be much easier to manage and scale later on. I've done flips in other states, but I don't advise it when you're starting out. If your local market fits all the previous criteria, then you're ready to go!

    If your local market does not fit our criteria, then it would be more beneficial to look into other markets. Find the closest city that meets all the criteria above and set up shop there. It will be harder to set up, but it will be more profitable than staying in your current market. Hopefully you can find an ideal market within a two-hour drive.

Choosing your market is very important. You can have everything in place, but if you're in the wrong market, it will make it harder to succeed. Choose a market that fits all the criteria and you will be set up for success.

CHAPTER 5:

The Dream Team

After choosing your market, it's time to assemble the Dream Team. This team will consist of *Real Estate Agents, Contractors, Lenders,* and *Escrow Officers*. Notice how all those people are plural. You never want to rely on just one person for anything. You need to be searching for multiple people in each category.

So how do you find these people? The first thing you do is post on Facebook and social media that you're looking for real estate agents, contractors, lenders, and escrow officers. You'll be surprised at how many of your friends know someone.

The next strategies will explain how to find each type of team member.

Real Estate Agents

Most real estate agents will not be willing to do what we need. You're going to be giving them search criteria that seem unrealistic to them. They will tell you you're crazy and you'll never get a deal like that. I still get Realtors who laugh at me or scold me for making such low offers. That's fine with me. It means I'll get more deals since they don't know what's possible.

So where do we find the real estate agents who know what we need? The place is your local real estate investing group. You can find these on Meetup.com or by Googling "(your city) REIA". REIA stands for Real Estate

Investing Association, and they're nationwide. The real estate agents who attend those events will be on the same page as you.

While you're at these events, you'll be around other house flippers. You can ask them for real estate agent referrals as well. Most people at these events are friendly and want to help each other. So often times they'll be happy to give you a referral.

Another way to find real estate agents is on Zillow. You're able to go through profiles to see how an agent is rated. I would ignore the top-rated agents because they will be too busy for what you need. Search for an agent in the middle of pack. That means they're active, but they'll be able to devote time to you.

Once you have narrowed down the target agents, you will send them an email. A lot of agents don't pick up their phone because they're showing properties or with clients. It's also time consuming to call all of them. So writing an email is easier for both parties. You'll send the following message:

"Hi, my name is _____. I'm a real estate investor and I'm looking for an agent to make offers for me on discounted properties. If you're willing to write a lot of offers, please give me a call at your earliest convenience."

If they contact you back after that email, then they should make a good candidate for your team. The most time-consuming portion for the agent will be writing up offers and showing properties. It's impossible to get deals unless you're consistently making offers. Most agents aren't willing to do this because most of the offers we make will be low. So when you find an agent who is willing to, you know they're a keeper.

You'll be relying on these agents to sell your property when it's complete. This is why you need to have multiple agents on your team. They all may charge different commissions and provide different services for your listings. It's also good to get different agents' opinions on what a property is worth. One agent might know a particular area really well and have better insight. So network with as many agents as possible and build up your Dream Team roster.

Contractors

As I said earlier, I am not handy at all. I didn't know anything about construction when I started and I still wouldn't call myself an expert today. The good thing is you shouldn't be doing any construction yourself. You're a real estate investor, not a contractor. Even if you're handy and you know how to fix homes, you shouldn't be fixing them yourself. You can only fix so many homes at the same time. If you want to flip more houses, hire contractors to do it. Your time should be spent looking for more deals and growing your business. Keep things simple, don't pick up a hammer!

Now, when talking to contractors, you need to be very clear with them about your expectations. Let them know you're an investor flipping houses and that you don't pay retail pricing. A lot of contractors won't want to work with you after that. That's alright! We're trying to save time for everybody, so it's better to be honest from the start.

The ones who say they're OK with investor pricing are the people we want. Let them know you plan on buying multiple homes. Also tell them if their work is good and their pricing is fair, they will get more jobs. Then, ask them if they currently have a job they're working on. If they do, then go see it and check out the quality of their work. Ask them for before and after pictures from previous jobs. Contractors should always have these! If they don't, then I wouldn't trust them to do work for me. It means they're either inexperienced or not very smart. In any case, I don't want to hire them.

Lastly, ask them for previous client referrals. They should be willing to give you at least one person who they've done work for. Call that person up and see what they think. Typically, if the contractor gave you their info, then their client will probably have positive things to say about them.

But it all just shows the contractor is on top of their game. If they're willing to take you to a job site, show you before and after pictures, and give you their client's number, then you should give that contractor a shot.

So the question is how do you find contractors?

1. **Home Depot.** Talk with the Pro Desk and ask them if they know of any contractors who come in a lot. Let them know you flip houses and that you need more crews. Also take note of all the people going in and out. If they look like contractors, go talk to them and get their information. I heard a good tip from another investor that you should go to Home Depot early in the morning. You'll find all the contractors who are getting up early and working. That doesn't mean they'll be good or fairly priced, but it is a good thing that they're working early.

2. **Referrals.** Contractor referrals are a bit harder to get than other referrals. If an investor has a good one, they very rarely will give them up. Mainly because they need them and don't want them to get busy on someone else's job. It doesn't hurt to ask, but don't be surprised if you get turned down.

3. **Google, Yelp, and Craigslist.** If you search "Las Vegas contractors" in Google or Yelp, you'll probably get a list of bigger companies. They will likely be more expensive than their competitors. I'm usually not going to be interested in these companies. I'm more interested in the companies on the second and third page of Google. Give them a call and see if they're a potential fit.

4. **Dumpster Driving.** I know what you're thinking, it sounds like dumpster "diving." But it's "driving." When I'm driving around the city, I'm always on the lookout for the big dumpsters you have to rent. If there's a dumpster in the front yard or the street, that means there is probably a contractor working on that home. When I see that, I stop at the house and knock on the door. If they answer, I let them know I'm a real estate investor looking for more contractors. I then ask them if they're looking for more work. If they say yes, then I will ask for a tour of the house.

Now I can see the quality of work and ask them ask them more questions. This is one of my best strategies for finding good contractors!

Those are all the ways I find contractors. Always be looking for more even if you don't have work for them yet. Hopefully you'll run into the problem of having so many flips that you don't have enough contractors. That means you're getting a lot of deals!

Lastly, understand that you're going to lose contractors as you go along. Some are going to get tired of you, some won't like the pay, and others might find another investor they think is better. It's just part of this business, so always be looking for more contractors.

Lenders

If you remember, my false belief was that I needed more money. I thought it would be so hard to find the cash to buy a property. I later learned that finding money is not hard!

There are two types of lenders: Professional and Private. A professional lender would be a company that funds deals. A private lender would be a normal person who wants to lend. This can be anyone, but typically a private lender already knows and trusts you. So how do you find each?

Professional Lenders

Starting out, you're most likely going to use professional lenders. If you don't have a track record of flipping houses, it's going to be harder to convince your friends and family to invest. My first two years I only used professional lenders. After I finally proved myself, I got my first private lender. So don't be surprised if your friends don't trust you with their money yet.

The most common professional lender would be the big banks. This includes Wells Fargo, Chase, Bank of America, etc. They're great for long-term purchases like rentals and your personal residence. They're not going to work for flipping houses, though.

When you get a loan from them, it's typically 30 years with a low interest rate. That sounds great, but the problem is all the paperwork and restrictions.

1. They need to run your credit and get your tax returns, bank accounts, pay stubs, and other documents.

2. You need a certain Debt-to-Income Ratio to prove you can make the monthly payments.

3. You'll have to come up with a Down Payment. It can't be from someone else.

4. You need to pay for an Appraisal.

5. Usually the property has to be in "livable" condition to qualify for the loan.

6. It will take 30 to 45 days to close the loan.

All of these hurdles make it very difficult to flip houses with that type of loan. Also, you'll be competing with people offering cash who will buy as is and close in less than 14 days. Sellers are going to take the quick money the majority of the time. So if that's not going to work, then what should you do?

Search for Hard Money Lenders. A Hard Money Lender is someone who specializes in investment properties. They make their living off funding house flippers.

1. They can close in less than 14 days, as with cash.

2. Some don't require appraisals, and they understand you're buying property that is in rough shape.

3. They're not concerned with your credit score or tax returns.

They make an ideal lender for what we need. The big banks' major concern is you, the borrower. They're not as worried about the actual deal. A hard money lender is most concerned about the deal. They don't care about your credit score or tax returns. If you're getting a great deal, then they'll be good either way. If you sell the property, they'll make their money; if you default on the loan, then they'll get a property with a ton of equity in it.

So you're probably thinking to yourself, *What's the catch?* I learned a long time ago that if something sounds too good to be true, then it probably is. So here's the catch:

1. **Higher Costs.** At the time of this writing, the interest rates with big banks are around 4%. Most hard money lenders are 8% to 13%. They also charge 2 to 6 points on top of that. A point is an upfront cost you pay for the loan, and is equal to 1% of the total loan. So if you get a loan for $100,000, a point would be $1,000. If you pay 4 points up front, you would need to come up with $4,000 plus the monthly interest and the down payment.

2. **Shorter Loan Term.** With the big banks, you can get a 30-year loan. With hard money, it's usually a 6- to 12-month loan. That can be scary to think about. But, you shouldn't hold the properties longer than that anyway. My average flip last year was about four months from the day I bought it to the day it sold. So don't fear the short-loan term.

Now you know the pros and cons of hard money lenders. They are expensive, but if they allow you to buy a great deal, it's worth it.

They also provide another line of defense against buying a bad deal. You have to prove to them that it's a good deal when you apply. To do this, you send your comps and repair costs (we'll go over what comps and repair costs are in the following chapters). Sometimes they won't approve the loan because they see the numbers differently. You might think the house will sell for $200,000 while they think it will only sell for $160,000. So they deny your loan.

This is actually a good thing! They make money on giving loans, and if they turn down the chance to make money, then it tells you that it's a bad deal. So they provide a second set of eyes in addition to giving you money.

Both types of professional lenders have their strengths and weaknesses. I believe that hard money is the best route to go if you want to flip houses.

How to Find Hard Money Lenders

Finding hard money lenders is fairly simple. If you search online for local hard money lenders, you will get a bunch of results. There will be nationwide hard money lenders and others will be locally based ones. Typically, the nationwide ones will have lower fees and interest rates, but they will be harder to work with. The local hard money lenders might cost a little more, but they will be more personal and you can build a relationship with them. The local ones will have more flexibility to do different types of deals as well. However, it's important to have both nationwide and local hard money lenders. If one of them won't fund a certain deal, then you'll need to have a back up who will.

Private Lenders

Private lenders are typically friends or family members. It could be anyone with some money who wants to invest. Before you look for money, you need to decide how much money you want to put in the deal. I believe you should aim to have no money in every deal. I rarely put my own money in deals anymore because I have a lot of private lenders. I would rather save my cash for other opportunities such as rental properties.

There are two ways I structure deals with private lenders: *profit sharing or interest payments.*

Profit Sharing

Usually with this structure, you would find the deal and do all the work to get it flipped. Your lender would fund the deal and you both would split the profit at the end.

An example would be you go to your relative and say, "Let's split the profit 50/50. I'll find the deal and do all the work, while you provide all the money."

I see this type of deal worked out all the time. The profit split percentage might be different, but the idea is the same.

Interest Payments

In this structure, you will make monthly interest payments just like to a hard money lender, but you can get more creative with it. Instead of paying 12% and points, you can offer to pay whatever your lender is looking for. Maybe it's only 6% to 8%. A lot of people would love to get a 6% to 8% return on their money!

You could also structure it so that they get all their interest on the back end. That means you don't pay them any interest payments until the property sells. This allows you to save your cash and keep all the profit minus the interest. This is the route I go with my private lenders because it gives me the most upside. There have been times when I misjudged a project and my lender made more than me. But I'm OK with that! If we're both making money, then it's a good thing!

How to Get Private Money

The first thing you'll need to work on is your pitch. Why should people give you money? If you've never done a deal before, it will be harder to get people to invest. It's not impossible, but don't get too excited unless you have a rich uncle! In order to get people to invest, you need to be able to answer two questions for them:

Why should I trust you?

My response: **"I've purchased over 100 homes and I've been in real estate for nine years. Check out my website to see all my properties."**

What can you do for me?

My response: **"I can get you a 10% return on your money and it will be secured by real estate. This is a much better investment than the 0.0000001% (exaggeration, I know) you get at the bank. It's also a lot better than what you're getting in the stock market right now."**

Two simple responses to the two important questions. Of course, I will go in to more detail about the specifics of my business and our success. The point is to have a game plan with your pitch. The majority of you reading this book won't have that type of experience so your pitch will be different. You have to brainstorm and think about what you have done.

Your credentials are probably better than you think. Have you ever owned a home? If you have, then you're a real estate investor. Have you ever painted walls or done any type of work on a home? If you have, then you have experience in renovating homes. Are you reading this book? Then you've spent money and time to educate yourself to become a better real estate investor.

There are ways to give your pitch so that you look your best. When I started flipping full time, I told people I had flipped "multiple" homes. They didn't have to know that "multiple" only meant two. I would tell them I was "planning on doing 20 flips this coming year!" I ended up only buying five, but I wanted to buy 20! I wasn't lying when I would tell people that. So think about how you can sell yourself to other people in the best possible light.

The other important thing to know is how others perceive you. Have you been the type of person who is in and out of trouble? Are you someone with good morals who works hard?

If your friends and family know you're someone who isn't trustworthy, then there's no way they'll invest with you. If that's the case, then it's time to make a change. Regardless of what you've done, it's never too late to make a change. You're going to be creating a new life for yourself through real estate. Who cares what your old life was like? You have an opportunity to show people your new path.

The best way to do that is through social media. People think social media is reality more than actual reality is! It's stupid, but you can use that to your advantage. Start posting about all the things you're doing in real estate. It can be pictures of a house you went and looked at. It could be about a meeting you had with a real estate agent. Better yet, it could be about how you're reading this new awesome book!

No matter how big or small the event is, you should be posting about it. People will start associating you with real estate. Their trust in you will start to build. Then it will really take off once you buy your first flip!

You can create so much content from one flip! Every single milestone can be documented:

1. Seeing it for the first time.
2. Getting your offer accepted.
3. Buying it.
4. Getting bids for the renovation.
5. Picking a contractor.
6. Starting demolition.
7. Weekly progress pictures of the renovation.
8. Befores and afters when it's done.
9. Putting it on the market.
10. Getting offers.
11. Finally, selling it.

Creating content is not that hard. You just need to be willing and determined to document every detail along the way. If you do that, it will build people's trust in you. Once you build the trust, they will be more willing to invest with you!

Escrow Officer

The last member of the Dream Team will be your escrow officer. An escrow officer is someone who works for a Title Company. The Title Company is where you'll run the transaction through. They'll be responsible for distributing the money and exchanging the property. Some states use attorneys for this process as well.

I buy most of my properties in Nevada and we use Title Companies. They handle everything for the transaction so there are no attorneys involved. When I purchased a duplex in New York, we used an attorney along with the Title Company. So do your research and see what your state requires.

Once you get a property under contract, you will send it over to the Title Company. They will run a Preliminary Title Report. The title report will show the ownership history, liens, and other information about the home.

After you purchase the home, they will give you title insurance. Title insurance covers you for various reasons. A creditor might try to claim they're owed money from the previous owner. The Title Company would step in and fix it. They would also cover you if someone tried to dispute that you actually own the home.

This might seem crazy, but if somewhere along the way there was a fraudulent exchange of the property, then it could affect you. So it's always wise to go through a Title Company and get Title Insurance.

You also should always choose a nationwide Title Company. The nationwide companies have been around for a long time. So they should be around if anything happens later on. I'm not a fan of small local Title

Companies. If they go out of business, then you don't have title insurance anymore. So always choose the bigger companies if you can.

The next question is how do you choose which Title Company and Escrow Officer? There are three things I look for:

1. Are they going to mess up any of my deals?

I've seen many deals get killed by Title Companies for various reasons. The most common is they can't get the deal closed quickly enough. I've had deals where we need to close in a couple of days, because the seller is in foreclosure. I need a Title Company that can put that at the top of their priority list and make sure it closes.

I've had other times where a Title Company didn't want to do the deal because they didn't like the fee someone was getting paid. A deal can get messed up for the silliest reasons! So make sure your Title Company is doing everything they can to make the transaction as easy as possible.

2. How responsive are they?

I've dealt with some escrow officers who only respond via email. They won't give their cell phone number and they never answer their office phone! I don't want to deal with those types of people. Some escrow officers have the mindset that they only work Monday to Friday, 9 to 5. If it's not within those hours, they're not responding.

It's standard to follow that protocol, but I want the people who go above and beyond. I want the people who are as hungry as me to do deals! My escrow officer and I have an open line of communication. We'll call or text anytime. It doesn't matter if it's nights or weekends. She understands my needs and in return she gets a lot of business! Find someone who is responsive, because it's important to get deals closed.

3. **Are they going to give me investor discounts and not charge "junk fees"?**

Most Title Companies will have an investor discount. You usually have to ask in order to get it. Some Title Companies require you to have bought over three properties in the last year in order to qualify. Don't be surprised if that's the case. If they don't offer an investor discount, then you might want to look elsewhere.

The other way Title Companies make money is through "junk fees." They'll be disguised as Doc Prep Fees, Overnight Fees, Endorsement Fees, Notary Fees, and so on. They can add up quickly and cost you thousands throughout the year! Some of these fees are standard in the industry. but that doesn't mean you have to pay them. If you're bringing a high volume of deals, you have the ability to negotiate those fees out. If they won't remove them, then take your business somewhere that will.

Those are the three things I look for in a Title Company. If you can find one that does all three well, then keep them happy! If you have one that does the first two well but their fees are a little high, that's OK! I would rather pay more to make sure I get all my deals pushed through! It does you no good to pay low fees on a deal that gets killed. It also doesn't do you any good if I can't get ahold of the escrow officer. I'll happily pay higher fees for better service. So look for the ones who do at least the first two well.

Now the question is, how do you find them?

Escrow officers are the easiest members of the Dream Team to find. If you're in the industry, they will be trying to get your business. Even if you're a beginner, they will do whatever it takes to get your business.

The methods of finding them are the same as how you found other members of the Dream Team. Look on Google and Yelp, go to real estate investing groups, check Facebook, and ask other investors for referrals. You can also ask your real estate agents and lenders what title companies they like using. Here are the questions you need to ask when interviewing escrow officers:

1. Do you work with house flippers? (The answer should be "yes.")

2. What kind of investor discounts do you have? (There should be some type of discount.)

3. What's the quickest you can close a deal? (The answer should be four days or sooner.)

4. Can I contact you outside of work hours? (The answer should be "yes.")

5. How can you improve my business? (This could go a bunch of different ways. But it shows how creative they are if they can come up with ideas on the spot).

If they answer these questions correctly, then give them a chance. You never know how good someone is until you try them. I've had a lot of people talk a big game only to find out they couldn't produce. Find as many escrow officers as you can and try them out until you find the ones you like.

Dream Team Conclusion

You should understand why you need a Dream Team. Each member has their own purpose for helping you flip houses. When you start out, it's OK to only have one of each member. Your team will grow as you grow.

When I started out, I was my own real estate agent. I got a contractor referral from one of my friends. I found a hard money lender on Google. My escrow officer was referred by my mom. So it only took me a couple days to find my initial team.

With just that team, I was able to do deals. It took me years to grow my team to what it is now. I spent a long time figuring out how to find more members. It should be a much faster process for you now that you know exactly what to look for!

Searching for more team members should never prevent you from searching for more deals. Deals are the life blood of your business. You don't need a giant team unless you're doing a lot of deals. If you've got one person in each profession for your Dream Team, then you're ready to go! Worry about finding more Dream Team members once you have the deals to support more.

CHAPTER 6:

Evaluating Deals

Deal evaluation is the most important aspect of flipping houses. I see too many people get into bad deals because they don't understand the deal evaluation formula. When you watch the TV shows, they usually show the following formula:

Sale Price – Purchase Price – Renovation Cost – Realtor Fees = Profit

I thought that was the formula when I first started. I didn't realize all the costs that flipping a home really has. I was lucky I didn't sell my first home until two years later. If I would've tried to flip it immediately, I would have lost money. I don't want that to happen to you, so here is the real formula:

Sale Price – Purchase Price – Repair Costs – Realtor Fees – Holding Costs – Money Costs – Closing Costs – Other Fees = Profit

The first thing you're probably saying to yourself is, "There are a lot more costs than I thought!" I know when I first learned the formula, I was thinking that. Most people don't realize there are all these extra costs. By the time they finish the flip, they realize they didn't make any money! Here are the definitions of each variable.

Sale Price

This is what the home ends up selling for.

Purchase Price

How much you buy the home for.

Repair Costs

The total cost of all the repairs to the home.

Realtor Fees

How much you paid out to the Realtors.

Holding Costs

The cost of the property taxes, insurance, and utilities while you owned the property.

Money Costs

How much you paid your lenders for the money.

Closing Costs

All the fees and transfer tax paid at the Title Company.

Other Fees

These could be wholesaler fees (which we'll talk about later) or any other miscellaneous fees not covered in the formula.

Profit

How much you made after all that work!

Now you can properly evaluate deals, but we need to go over the order in which to do so. Most people will look at the asking price of the home and work from there. This is the wrong way to do it! At the end of the day, the asking price is almost irrelevant to us. It helps us know what the seller is thinking, or if we're even close on a deal, but it doesn't affect our calculations. All that matters is our *Max Offer*. Here is the formula to determine your *Max Offer*:

ARV – Repair Costs – Money Costs – Realtor Costs – Holding Costs – Closing Costs – Minimum Profit = Max Offer

Now let's discuss each part of the formula and how to calculate it.

ARV (After Repair Value)

ARV is your After Repair Value. This is what you project to sell the home for once the renovations are complete. It is the most important aspect of evaluating deals. If you get this wrong, then it could kill all your profit. So the question, is how do you calculate it?

Ideally you would have access to the MLS. The MLS is the Multiple Listing Service that Realtors use to see current homes for sale. You can also look at past home sales and homes currently under contract to be sold. If you don't have the MLS, you can still look on websites such as Redfin. com, Zillow.com, and Realtor.com. The MLS will have better data than any of those.

When we determine our ARV, we want to look at recent Sold Properties, Contingent Properties, and Active Properties. You need to find the most similar properties when looking at the sales. This is called comping out the property.

Sold Properties

Sold Properties are homes that have already sold. I don't like to look past three months, but I will look up to six months if there aren't a lot of comps. I'm going to put more weight on the most recent sales when I evaluate them.

We'd like our comps (comparable properties) to be within 20% of the square footage of the home. You should also compare homes with the same number of stories. I don't want to compare a two story home with a one story home unless I have no other option.

You also need to compare similar years built. Usually this will be within 10 years. The homes should also be close to the property, ideally in the same subdivision or block. If the next block over has the same type of homes in the same school district, then usually they can be used.

I don't like to use comparable homes that are across main streets because it can get you in trouble. In some states, the same exact house across the street could be worth significantly more because it's in a different school district.

Contingent Properties

Contingent Properties already have an accepted offer on the property, but it hasn't closed yet. They're good for adding support to what the Past Sales show us. You shouldn't ever use Contingent Sales as the sole justification for your ARV. There's always a chance that the buyer backs out. If that happens, you have nothing to base your value on.

I use Contingent Properties to see my upside. Maybe all the Sold Properties are $100,000 but there is a Contingent Property at $110,000. I will have my ARV at $100,000, but know that I could possibly have a $110,000 ARV by the time I hit the market. I must still buy the deal based on the $100,000 ARV. Having the possibility for a higher potential ARV could make it a great deal, though.

Active Properties

Active Properties are those currently on the market that have not accepted an offer. They don't do much to determine ARV, but they show you what your competition will be like when you list yours. If there are a lot of Active Properties like yours, then it will take longer to sell. If there are few Active Properties, then yours should sell quicker. So use that data to help determine your Holding Costs.

Other Factors

Besides looking at the different types of properties, there are other factors that determine ARV. The finishes in the home play a big role. Is the home in terrible, average, or newly renovated condition? If you plan on renovating the home, then you need to know what the renovated homes are selling for. Don't be concerned with the terrible or average homes because you won't be selling them.

You also want to know how many bedrooms, bathrooms, and garages are in the home. If you can find homes that are exactly the same as yours, then that's perfect! More likely though, you'll need to adjust your value based on the differences. If your home is three bedrooms and one bathroom, then you're probably not getting as much as the home with three bedrooms and two bathrooms.

Also, realize that two-bedroom homes are usually worth significantly less than three-bedroom homes. If you do have a two-bedroom home, you should be comparing it to other two-bedroom homes for your comps.

Other factors to consider when looking for comps are pools, lot size, and location. Homes with pools and bigger lots are usually going to be worth more. In some areas, though, pools are not desirable and they may not add any value! You have to know what your market values them at.

Take into account the location of your home. Is it on a main street? Does it have views? Is there a shopping center behind it? If it's in a golf course community, is it on the course? The value of your home can be significantly different than the comps because of its unique location. That's why it is always best to find the most similar properties in all aspects.

Example

Let's go through an example of how to calculate ARV. This was a property I made an offer on. I ran what's called a CMA (Comparative Market Analysis), and you can see what it looks like from the graphic that comes next.

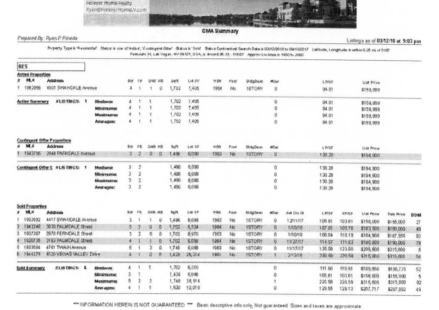

Active Properties

4501 Swandale Avenue is the property I'm evaluating. It's a four-bedroom, two-bathroom, single-story home built in 1964. The property is in rough shape, so I would plan on selling it fully renovated.

Sold Properties

4417 Swandale Avenue is 200 square feet smaller, one bedroom less, and sold for $155,000 three months ago. It's in bad condition. *It's not relevant to me, because I'm looking for renovated properties. We can toss this one out.*

3020 Palmdale Street is a model match with one more bedroom, and it sold for $183,000 two months ago. It's in average condition. *This tells me I should get at least $183,000, since my property will be fully renovated. The fifth bedroom this comp has doesn't add that much value in this neighborhood.*

2978 Ferndale Street is a model match with one less bedroom that sold for $187,550 two months ago. It's in average condition. *This tells me I* *should get more than $187,550, since my property is renovated and has one more bedroom.*

3183 Palmdale Street is also a model match with the same number of bedrooms, and it sold for $190,000 three months ago. It's a renovated home. *This is an example of a perfect comp. Everything is the same and it has been renovated. This tells me I should expect to get $190,000 as well.*

4761 Twain Avenue is about the same size, with one more bedroom and bathroom. It sold for $215,000 four months ago. It's a renovated home. *I'm intrigued by this. It's a little farther away and it has one more bedroom and bathroom. But it sold for $25,000 more than my model match comp above. This makes me think I could possibly have more upside than the $190,000.*

4520 Vegas Valley Drive is about 300 square feet smaller but the lot is almost four times the size. It only has one bathroom and one garage. It sold for $315,000 one month ago. It's a renovated home. *This home is not a comp at all. The home is smaller, but the lot is just so much bigger. A property like this is too different than mine because of the lot.*

Contingent Properties

2944 Parkdale Avenue is 200 square feet smaller and has one less bathroom. It's under contract to sell, with a list price of $194,000. It's a renovated home. *This hasn't sold yet, so we don't know what it will eventually sell for. But we have a good idea that it might sell for $194,000. If it does, that's a good thing, because my home is bigger and has more bathrooms. So I should be able to get more than this, but only if it sells for that price.*

ARV Conclusion

Based on all these comps, I would safely say my ARV is $190,000. I give the most weight to the comp on 3183 Palmdale Street, because it is an exact match for what mine will be. Some of the comps sold for slightly less but they were in worse condition than what mine will be.

I have a comp that sold for $215,000 and I could possibly have a Contingent Property sell for $194,000. Based on those two, I have some upside to possibly get $200,000 or more. When evaluating the deal, I would offer based on a $190,000 ARV. If it gets more then it's a home run.

ARV is tough to calculate in the beginning. The only way to improve is to practice and evaluate more deals. Have a real estate agent on your Dream Team double-check your work. If they think it's different, ask them why. Feedback and practice are going to help you get better determining the ARV.

P/Sq Ft Method

Some people like to calculate ARV using P/Sq Ft (Price per Square Foot Method). It is very misleading, and I see a lot of people try to use it to justify their ARV.

To do this, they take the P/Sq Ft of a small home and then take the square footage of their bigger home, and multiply it to get their ARV. An example would look like this:

Home A is 1,000 square feet and sold for $100,000. You get the P/Sq Ft by taking $100,000 (price) and dividing it by 1,000 (square feet). That equals $100/Sq Ft.

Home B is 2,000 square feet. Since **Home A's** P/Sq Ft is $100, that means Home B's ARV should be $200,000. We get this by taking the 2,000 square feet and multiplying it by $100.

In the real world this never actually works. Homes usually get cheaper per square foot as they get bigger. If you don't believe me, go look at newly built homes and check out their P/Sq Ft on their models. Usually the P/Sq Ft goes down as the square footage goes up. That has to do with the cost of building the home. The initial hard costs of the land, permits, foundation, plumbing, and other factors get lower as you build bigger.

Don't fall into the trap of thinking you'll get the same P/Sq Ft as another property that is a lot bigger or smaller. Use the methods we learned, and you will be more accurate when calculating ARV.

Repair Costs

Repair Costs are the second most difficult aspect to figure out. When I first started, I don't think I ever got one right. I would walk through homes and think every property was a $20,000 rehab! I didn't take into account the size of the property. If it looked like it needed a good amount of work, then I was guessing the rehab was $20,000. Obviously, that wasn't very smart of me. I made mistakes from buying deals that I thought would cost $20,000 but ended up being $35,000.

I also missed out on potential deals where the rehab would've been $12,000 but I thought it was $20,000. As I started flipping more properties, I began to understand how to accurately estimate my Repair Costs. I started to see what granite counters, kitchen cabinets, carpet, tile, and all my other prices were. That allowed me to walk into properties and price everything out piece by piece.

It's hard to get to that point from the beginning, because it takes a lot of experience. One thing you can do is ask your contractors if they have a price sheet for each repair. It would have every detail on there such as sink, faucet, windows, and doors. You could then walk the house and mark as you go along. Once you get through the whole property, you can add up all the repairs for an accurate budget.

Not everyone has that option, though. Luckily, there is another way that is much easier. It's the P/Sq Ft Method but for rehab costs. We went over the reasons not to use that for determining ARV, but it is very effective for determining rehab costs. The figures given next are for what I've seen as a general guideline for contractors. Every market is different, so don't take these figures as set in stone. You may have to adjust based on your area.

Clean-Up Rehab: $5 to $10 P/Sq Ft

This would be a very light rehab. It would include paint, carpet, and small repairs. With jobs this small, you can't really put an exact P/Sq Ft on it. What needs to be done is going to vary considerably if it's this small.

Lipstick Rehab: $15 P/Sq Ft

The lipstick remodel is exactly how it sounds. We're going to be keeping a lot of the things in the property and putting some lipstick on them. A typical rehab for this would include paint, tile or laminate flooring, granite counters, kitchen cabinet refinishing, small bathroom remodel, and slight landscaping.

Full Interior Rehab: $20 P/Sq Ft

This would be replacing everything inside. Paint, tile or laminate flooring, granite counters, new kitchen cabinets, full bathroom remodels, and slight landscaping.

Full Rehab: $25 P/Sq Ft

This would be everything the Full Interior Rehab includes, but it adds a large-expense item such as the AC, roof, or pool. If it needs two of the large-expense items, figure $30 P/Sq Ft. If you need all three big expenses, then plan for $35 P/Sq Ft!

This is the way to quickly calculate rehab costs. I use this method when I'm evaluating deals I haven't seen in person. I evaluate so many deals each day that it is impossible to see them all. This method will give you a good idea on the costs, but it will not be exact. As you start doing more deals you'll be able to get more accurate and price each item out.

Anytime you can, bring a contractor with you. Have them explain to you what each repair will cost as you walk through the home. This will be a great learning experience and you'll be able to have an accurate bid on that property.

Always use the P/Sq Ft method if you can't get access to a contractor that day or if you can't see the property in person.

Money Costs

ARV and Repair Costs are the most difficult components to calculate because they vary with every property. The rest of these costs are easy to account for. Money Costs are what your lender charges you. If you're using your own cash, then your Money Costs will be $0. Most of the time, you're going to use lenders to fund your deals.

In the Dream Team section, we went over Hard Money Lenders and Private Lenders. With Private Lenders, Money Costs are going to vary on what they charge you. The Hard Money Lender rates are similar, usually 8% to 13% interest and 2 to 6 points up front.

When calculating your costs, you need to know your hold time. I know my average hold time for properties is four months. Your market may be different, so you need to figure out your hold time from the beginning.

To calculate your hold time, you look at the *DOM* (Days on Market). This tells you how many days it took before they accepted an offer. It doesn't take into account how long it took for the buyer to close on the property. A buyer getting a loan will take 30-45 days to close. A cash buyer should take around 14 days to close.

Looking back at our example from the *ARV* section, you can see the DOM on the right side.

Ryan Pineda
Forever Home Realty
Ryan@ForeverHomeLV.com

CMA Summary

Prepared By: Ryan P Pineda

Listings as of **03/12/18 at 9:03 pm**

Property Type is "Residential" Status is one of "Active", "Contingent Offer" Status is "Sold" Status Contractual Search Date is 03/12/2016 to 09/13/2017 Latitude, Longitude is within 0.25 mi of 0.0007 Palmdale St, Las Vegas, NV 89121, USA, is around 38, 13, 149.27 Approx Liv Area is 1600 to 2000

RES

Active Properties

#	MLS #	Address	Bdr	FB	3/4B	HB	SqFt	Lot SF	Y/Blt	Pool	BldgDesc	#Gar	L Price	List Price
1	1962956	4501 BRANDALE Avenue	4	1	1	0	1,792	7,405	1984	No	1STORY	0	94.01	$159,999

Active Summary:	# LISTINGS:	1	Median:	4	1	1		1,792	7,405				0	94.01	$159,999
			Minimum:	4	1	1		1,792	7,405				0	94.01	$159,999
			Maximum:	4	1	1		1,792	7,405				0	94.01	$159,999
			Average:	4	1	1		1,792	7,405				0	94.01	$159,999

Contingent Offer Properties

#	MLS #	Address	Bdr	FB	3/4B	HB	SqFt	Lot SF	Y/Blt	Pool	BldgDesc	#Gar	L Price	List Price
1	1943295	2044 PALMDALE Avenue	3	2	0	0	1,496	6,098	1963	No	1STORY	0	130.28	$194,900

Contingent Offers Summary:	# LISTINGS:	1	Median:	3	2			1,496	6,098				0	130.28	$194,900
			Minimum:	3	2			1,496	6,098				0	130.28	$194,900
			Maximum:	3	2			1,496	6,098				0	130.28	$194,900
			Average:	3	2			1,496	6,098				0	130.28	$194,900

Sold Properties

#	MLS #	Address	Bdr	FB	3/4B	HB	SqFt	Lot SF	Y/Blt	Pool	BldgDesc	#Gar	Act Cls Dt	L Price	$/SF	List Price	Sale Price	DOM
1	1932692	4417 BRANDALE Avenue	3	1	1	0	1,496	6,098	1963	No	1STORY	0	1/31/17	105.61	103.61	$158,000	$155,000	27
2	1942248	3020 PALMDALE Street	3	2	0	0	1,792	6,534	1964	No	1STORY	0	3/09/18	107.81	105.75	$193,900	$190,000	49
3	1937767	2970 FERNDALE Street	3	2	0	0	1,792	6,970	1963	No	1STORY	0	1/05/18	106.64	110.19	$184,900	$197,550	82
4	1936736	3163 PALMDALE Street	4	1	1	0	1,792	6,098	1964	No	1STORY	0	11/27/17	114.57	111.61	$185,000	$180,000	79
5	1933588	4761 TWAIN Avenue	5	1	2	0	1,748	5,698	1963	No	1STORY	0	11/17/17	120.00	123.00	$209,900	$215,000	5
6	1944270	4530 VEGAS VALLEY Drive	4	1	0	0	1,428	28,314	1981	Yes	1STORY	1	2/13/18	220.59	220.59	$315,000	$315,000	54

Sold Summary:	# LISTINGS:	6	Median:	4	1	1		1,792	6,316				0	111.60	110.91	$190,950	$196,775	52
			Minimum:	3	1			1,428	6,098				1	105.61	103.61	$158,000	$155,000	5
			Maximum:	5	2	2		1,748	28,314				1	220.59	220.59	$315,000	$315,200	82
			Average:	4	1	1		1,630	13,819				0	139.55	129.13	$207,717	$207,292	49

*** INFORMATION HEREIN IS NOT GUARANTEED *** Bases descriptive info only. Not guaranteed. Sizes and taxes are approximate.

It took 27, 49, 82, 79, 5, and 54 days to sell those six homes. All of those numbers won't apply, though. The comps you use for your ARV are the ones that are most important.

The three model match comps took 49, 82, and 79 days. The comp on 4761 Twain Avenue that sold for 215k and in 5 days is an outlier. You could get lucky and as quick as that, but don't plan on it. You should plan to sell in the 49 to 82 day range. For this home, you should take the average of the three model matches. That gives you a 70-day hold time.

Remember that this number doesn't include the time it takes for the buyer to close. So let's assume it takes them 45 days to do so. Now you're at 115 days to close. This is the time from putting it on the market to selling it.

The last thing to add is the rehab time. Rehab time is going to vary depending on how big the job is and how fast the contractor is. You'll have to get an idea from your contractor on the time frame. Keep in mind that contractors usually take longer than they quote you.

On this example let's say the rehab takes 60 days. If you take the 60 days for the rehab time and add it to the 115 days it takes to sell it, you get 175 days. So this property's hold time should be about 6 months.

The rest of our costs can be calculated with the hold time. Let's assume you're getting a Hard Money Loan at 11% interest and 4 points. The loan amount is $120,000.

Up front you will pay 4 points on the $120,000. A point is 1% of the loan amount. So 4 points on $120,000 would be $4,800. That is owed to the lender as an initial cost.

Then you have your monthly payments, which are annualized and interest only. At 11%, your monthly payment would be $1,100. Our hold time is 6 months, so the total cost of the monthly payments would be $6,600.

Take that $6,600 and add it to the points cost of $4,800. This gives us our Money Costs, which come out to be **$11,400**.

New investors don't realize how expensive Money Costs can be. They have to be accounted for when evaluating a deal. I've only lost money on one deal, and it was mainly because of Money Costs.

I bought a home for $535,000 and I thought it would sell within three months. I put it on the market and it didn't get any offers for two months. I took it off and spent $20,000 to rehab it. A few months later it finally sold for the ARV I anticipated.

I lost money because my hold time was 5 months longer and I spent $20,000 more in Repair Costs. The interest payments were about $5,000, so I was over budget by $25,000 on my Money Costs.

The loss ended up being about $20,000! My wallet didn't like it, but it was a great learning experience. The lesson here is always factor in your Money Costs.

Realtor Costs

When you put your Dream Team together, you should have an idea of what your Realtor will charge you to list a property. Technically, there is no standard commission according to the National Association of Realtors.

But the common commission fee is 6%. Half of that goes to the selling agent (the agent who brings the buyer) and the other half goes to your listing agent.

There are a lot of advertisements to list your home for 1%. These ads are misleading because they're only talking about the listing agent portion. You still need to decide what you want to pay the selling agent side. If you do a 1% listing, just know that it's really 4% if you pay the selling agent 3%.

Listing Agent Fee

Typically, the 1% listing agent is going to do the bare minimum for you. I like to think of them like the cheap airlines. You should get to your destination (hopefully), but don't expect any amenities! If you want someone to be hands on, provide great service, and be an awesome experience, then you're going to need to pay 2% to 3% on that side.

If you're starting out, you should get a Realtor who is going to put the time in with you so that you can learn the ropes. As you gain experience and do more flips, you can start naming your price for your listing agents.

Buyer's Agent Fee

What you decide to pay the selling agent is going to be important. The standard commission on their side is 3%. If you offer 1%, they're not going to show your property. I usually never offer less than 3% to the selling agent, because I want them motivated to bring me a buyer. I'll even offer 3.5% to 4% to a selling agent if I have a property that is taking a long time to sell! I know if a selling agent sees that, they're going to push their buyer to see your property. If their buyer is choosing between my property and a similar one, their agent will probably push for mine.

FSBO (For Sale By Owner)

I hear a lot of people say, "I don't need a Realtor! I can sell it on my own and save the 6%." I usually have two responses to that:

1. "Good Luck. Let me know how that works out for you."

2. "I can cut my own hair, but I would rather pay a professional to do it so I don't look like an idiot."

FSBO will usually cost you more money than you save. I have tried to market my own properties on sites like Craigslist and Zillow and it has never worked. The only people interested in my homes were other investors!

A big strategy for investors is to target FSBOs. So when the only offers are coming from investors, the property ends up selling for under market value. If you list it instead, you would net more money even after paying 6% to a Realtor.

The property will also sell much faster being listed on the MLS. That means your Money Costs go down because it sold quicker. Lastly the time wasted trying to sell it on your own is preventing you from finding the next deal. Do you want to miss out on a deal that would've made you $30,000 because you want to cut costs? I would rather let a professional handle the sale so I can get a higher price and find my next deal.

Realtor Costs Conclusion

Always plan on using a Realtor to sell your home. If you're a licensed Realtor, then you can list it yourself and save some money. I started out listing my own properties as well. I don't list my flips anymore, because it takes up too much of my time and prevents me from finding more deals. I pay a listing agent a smaller fee, because I give them a large volume of listings. If you're just starting out, you should have no problem listing your properties and finding your next deal.

If you're not licensed, then pay the 4% to 6% to list it with a Realtor. How much you pay will depend on your experience and what type of agent you work with. Know the cost beforehand so you can estimate your costs effectively.

Holding Costs

These are the property taxes, insurance, and utilities that occur while you own the home. They are pretty easy to look up and calculate.

Property Taxes can be looked up online. You can figure out how much that will be per month. Property Taxes are different than Transfer Tax. Property Taxes are paid every year. Transfer Tax is a one-time tax that is paid when the property is sold. Who will pay the Transfer Tax is always negotiated in the contract.

Insurance will be determined when you get your quote. You'll know how much that will be per month. Make sure you get insurance that covers vacant homes. It costs more, but it will be worth it if anything happens. If you get a normal policy and they find out it was vacant, you might have issues with a claim.

Utilities will vary based on a few factors. These factors are square footage, age of the home, time of year, lawn size, pool, and by city. People in California know how much more expensive water is than people in other states. I own a couple of cabins in Big Bear, California, and apparently they have the costliest water in the United States. My water bill for my 900 square foot cabin has been $800 some months!

There is no magic formula to calculate your utility costs. You'll have to use your knowledge from paying your own bills.

Closing Costs

These are the costs for the Title Company. This will cover escrow fees, Title Insurance, Transfer Tax, and other miscellaneous fees. Budget about 2% to 3% for closing costs to cover the purchase and sale of the property. It will vary depending on who pays what costs and what state you're in. If you plan for 3% of your ARV, you'll be covered. If it ends up being less, then it's extra profit!

Minimum Profit

This one is the easiest to calculate! What's the minimum profit you want to make? Take into account the amount of risk and time you're going to spend on this project. I adjust my Minimum Profit based on the deal. If I have a deal that's a Lipstick Rehab and I know I can sell it quick, I'll have a smaller Minimum Profit. If it's a property that's Full Rehab and going to take a long time to sell, my Minimum Profit will be higher because there is more risk and time. So many things can go wrong when you have bigger rehabs. For beginners, I recommend two guidelines:

1. Minimum Profit should not be under 10% of *ARV*.

2. Minimum Profit should not be under $20,000.

The first rule is to protect you from getting burned on bigger deals. If you have an ARV of $200,000, then your *Minimum Profit* should be $20,000. Making $20,000 on $200,000 is a nice deal. Making $20,000 on a $1,000,000 ARV is not a good deal! There is too much risk for a property that expensive. If the property only sells for $900,000, you would lose $80,000! Not a risk you want to take. If you're flipping a property that expensive, your minimum profit should at least be $100,000.

The second rule is to protect you from getting burned on the small deals. If you use the first rule and your ARV is only $100,000, then your *Minimum Profit* would only need to be $10,000. That's not enough to justify the risk and time it's going to take. If the rehab goes over budget $10,000, you have no profit. That's why your *Minimum Profit* should be at least $20,000. That will protect you in case you miscalculate ARV or Repair Costs.

Minimum Profit can be whatever you want. You might only want to do bigger deals with a Minimum Profit of $50,000. Those deals are harder to find, but they're definitely out there. Decide how much you want to make and then you can offer accordingly.

Max Offer Example

Here is the Max Offer formula again:

ARV – Repair Costs – Money Costs – Realtor Costs – Holding Costs – Closing Costs – Minimum Profit = Max Offer

We see the property *123 Main Street is* listed at $129,000. We do our research and figure out the *Repair Costs* are **$25,000,** the *ARV* is **$180,000**, and the hold time on the property should be **four months**. Knowing that, we can figure out the rest.

- *Money Costs* are three points plus 12% interest for four months. Your loan amount will depend on how large a down payment you put down and what the purchase price ends up being. For this example, we'll assume your loan is for $120,000. So $3,600 for points and $4,800 for interest. **$8,400**

- *Realtor Costs* are 5% of the $180,000 *ARV*. **$9,000**

- *Holding Costs* are $400 a month for four months. **$1,600**

- *Closing Costs* will be 3% of $180,000. **$5,400**

- *Minimum Profit* we want on this deal is **$20,000**.

Plug them in to determine our *Max Offer*:

$180,000 (ARV) − $25,000 (Repair Costs) − $8,400 (Money Costs) − $9,000 (Realtor Costs) − $1,600 (Holding Costs) − $5,400 (Closing Costs) − $20,000 (Minimum Profit) = **$110,600 (Max Offer)**

On this property, our *Max Offer* is **$110,600.** This is the most we're willing to pay. If we can get the property for less, then it's more profit!

In the example, the seller is asking $129,000. We're not where they want to be, but we might as well make the offer. You would be surprised how many sellers would take $100,000 in this situation. If you do all the work to evaluate the deal, then take the final step and make the offer. The worst that can happen is they say no.

That's everything you need to know about evaluating deals. Now we can transition to the fun part. How do you find the deals?

CHAPTER 7:
Free Leads

In order to find deals, you must first generate leads. A lead is any property you evaluate to buy. I buy less than 1% of the leads I evaluate. That's not a high percentage, so in order to do a lot of deals, you need a lot of leads. The goal is to build up as many lead sources as possible.

There are two types of leads: *Free Leads* and *Paid Leads.* A Free Lead doesn't cost money, but there is a cost in terms of your time. A Paid Lead costs money, but usually doesn't take as much of your time. When I first started, I didn't have a lot of money. I had a lot of time, so I focused on Free Leads.

As my business has grown, I've started to value my time more. So now I spend more money on Paid Leads. I incorporate both methods into my business so I can get as many leads as possible. For this chapter we'll focus on Free Leads.

1. *MLS Leads*

When I first started out, MLS Leads were the only way I knew how to find deals. I would browse and see if I saw anything interesting. A problem began to develop. I would look through the same properties over and over. It was really time consuming.

One day I realized I could set up auto searches. That was a game changer! I could set up any search I wanted, and I would automatically be emailed any new homes that popped up on that search. Learning about that feature was exciting, but I still needed to figure out the best way to use it. After lots of trial and error, I found the best auto searches that have led me to deals.

Zip Code Method

My favorite search is using the P/Sq Ft input in every zip code. Make sure you're only searching SFR (Single Family Residence). It can be done for condos and townhomes, but make sure that search is separate from the SFR search.

To do this search, start by inputting a zip code and look at the results. Sort the results by P/Sq Ft and start with the cheapest. Next, look at what the P/Sq Ft of the fifth one on the list is. That will be the P/Sq number you use for the search.

Set up the search by inputting the zip code and the P/Sq Ft number just found as the max. If done correctly, five results should pop up. It could be more if the P/Sq Ft for the fifth result was the same as the sixth result. But it should definitely not be less. If it's less or significantly more than five, then it was set up wrong.

Once you've mastered that process, you'll need to do that for every zip code you want to buy in. You can do this method for SFRs, Condos, and Townhomes, but you'll need to do them all in their own search. It is very time consuming to do, but the results will be worth it! You will know any time a discounted property in that zip code comes on the market.

If you really want to customize the search, you could do it the same way, but make it for Single Story and Two Story. Then you will have a Single Story Search and a Two Story Search for every zip code. It will provide better leads, but it's double the work to set up and maintain.

You could also do it on a block-by-block basis. If you know that certain blocks in the same zip code command higher prices, then you could set the search up to be Block Specific. It will take a lot more time to set one up for every block. Plus, you would need to have the knowledge of how blocks are valued differently.

No matter how you customize this search, it will need to be maintained in order to be effective. Check on it once a month to make sure your P/Sq Ft is still accurate for that zip code. In a market that's appreciating, you will not have enough results with the P/Sq Ft from a month ago. In a market that is depreciating, you will get too many results. Constantly check and make sure your P/Sq Ft yields around five results.

Keyword Method

This method is much easier to set up than the zip code method. It has led to deals for me but not nearly as many as the zip code method. To do this search, go to the Keywords Input and search words associated with good deals. Here are some examples:

Fixer, Fixer Upper, Needs Work, TLC, Investor, Short Sale Approved, Handyman, Motivated, Distressed.

You can come up with your other keywords as well. But that's all there is to this search!

DOM Method

Set up searches that notify you when a property has a certain number of DOM (Days on Market). I recommend searches of 45, 60, 75, 90, 105, and 120 DOM. The seller will start becoming more motivated the longer the property sits on the market. The first search would come up at 45 days on the market. Make an offer on the home and see if they're willing to make a deal.

Assuming they don't accept the offer and they can't sell the property, it will pop up on your 60 DOM search. Contact them again, and let them know your offer still stands. On day 75 it'll pop up again if they still haven't sold it.

This keeps happening until they make a deal with you or someone else. Your odds of getting the deal are higher because you've been contacting them. Most deals aren't made on the first try with any type of lead. It's the follow-ups that produce the deals.

Vacant Cash Method

Search for homes that are vacant and only accepting cash. This means the property is probably pretty beat up, since no one is living there, and they don't want any loan offers. It's a prime target for a flip!

Foreclosure Method

Search for properties that are in the foreclosure process. This is not the same as searching for properties that are REOs (Real Estate Owned) or Bank Owned. This search is for sellers who have been served an NOD (Notice of Default) and are in the process of being foreclosed on. They haven't paid their mortgage and they will lose the home soon. This search will produce highly motivated sellers.

MLS Leads Conclusion

These are the ways to find deals on the MLS. I use these methods because they work regardless of what the market is doing. They need to be consistently updated. Every day, I look through emails from my auto searches I have set up. It's a Free Lead source you need to take advantage of.

If you're a Realtor, set them up yourself. If you're not licensed, have an agent set them up for you. It is a lot of work to set up the zip code searches, so don't be surprised if an agent doesn't want to do it. If this is the case, find an agent who will or get access to the MLS so you can set them up yourself.

2. Wholesalers

You're probably thinking to yourself, *Is this guy talking about Costco?* That's what I thought the first time I heard about wholesalers in real estate.

I found out they weren't talking about Costco, but the guys who post those annoying signs everywhere saying "We Buy Houses!" I used to think the people who put them out were scammers. Then I learned that calling those signs could make me a lot of money! So what is a wholesaler?

Someone asked me a couple months ago to describe a wholesaler in the simplest terms. The best I could come up with is a "contract flipper." That is really all these guys do. They find a good deal and get it under contract. Instead of buying it themselves, they sell the contract to someone else for a fee. The technical term is they "assign" the contract to a new buyer for an "assignment fee." The new buyer purchases the property for what the wholesaler negotiated plus their assignment fee.

I had a hard time grasping this concept at first. Don't feel bad if you're confused right now. Here is an example of how this would work:

Bill **(wholesaler)** agrees to buy Tom's **(seller)** home for $150,000. Bill and Tom sign a Purchase Agreement. At this point Bill is the **buyer** on the contract. Bill then goes to Ryan **(house flipper)** and offers him the property for $160,000. Ryan runs all the numbers and agrees that he is willing to pay $160,000 for the property. Bill and Ryan sign an Assignment Agreement stating Ryan will pay Bill a $10,000 Assignment Fee. This agreement now makes Ryan the **buyer** on the contract. None of the original contract terms have changed other than the **buyer** being switched from Bill to Ryan. The house will still sell for $150,000, but Ryan will be paying Bill a $10,000 Assignment Fee on top of that.

The end result is that Bill makes $10,000 without ever having to buy the property; Ryan gets a good deal he can flip, and Tom gets the $150,000 he wanted. It's a win for everyone involved! You might be thinking to yourself, *This wholesaling thing sounds way easier! You don't need to have money to buy the property, contractors to fix it, or worry about selling it!* That's all true, but you have to spend money and time in order to find the deals. You have to risk money to market to sellers and find deals.

Side Note: All of these methods we go over for generating leads are geared for flipping houses. If the deal is good enough, you always have the option of wholesaling it to someone else. For the purposes of this book we will assume we're creating lead sources for you to buy as flips.

Finding wholesalers will be key to doing more deals. They have already done all the work! You just need to decide if you will pay the price for their deal. The hard part is finding good wholesalers. Many of them aren't accurate with their ARV or Repair Costs. They think the deal is good, but it's really not. Be ready for that when talking to them and evaluating their deals. Here are the different ways to find wholesalers:

1. *Bandit Signs*

Whenever you see any of those "We Buy Houses" signs on the streets, call them. I call them and say, "Hi, my name is Ryan and I'm a cash buyer. I saw your bandit sign and I just wanted to introduce myself and see if you had any deals you were wholesaling?" Most likely they will say no, but they will want to add you to their Buyer's List. Give them all your info for that and thank them.

2. *Billboards*

This is similar to the bandit signs, but instead it's "We Buy Houses" on a billboard. Do the same thing and call!

3. *Craigslist*

Jump on the real estate section of Craigslist and search "Wholesale" and "Wholesaler." I used this method to find my first wholesale deal. Ironically, the wholesaler ended up becoming one of my mentors and a good friend. He usually bought all his properties, but he didn't have the capital to buy that one at the time.

It ended up working out great for me. I got a good deal and a mentor! Be aware that most of the deals posted are usually fake. Wholesalers are taught to do that in order to build their Buyer's List. Don't get mad about it. Give them their info and stay in contact with them.

4. *REI Events*

Go on Meetup.com and search for your local REI events. You should already be at those events looking for members for your Dream Team. It's also a good way to find wholesalers! Any time you go to those events, make sure you network with everyone.

5. *Facebook Groups*

Search "Wholesale Real Estate Group" on Facebook and you will find a bunch of different wholesaling groups. There are nationwide groups and smaller local groups. Go ahead and join them all. Post where you're from and that you're a Cash Buyer looking for properties. Wholesalers will flock to you because a lot of new ones don't have anyone to sell to yet.

6. *Google Search*

Go online and search forms of "We Buy Houses," "Cash for Home," and "Home Cash Offer." Visit the top websites and contact them. Typically, these are all wholesalers. If they're popping up on the first page of Google, then they're paying a lot of money to get there. If they're spending a lot of money, hopefully they have deals they need to sell.

Wholesaler Conclusion

Wholesalers are an awesome Free Lead source to utilize. If you can network and find the best on es in your market, you will do a lot more deals. Don't look down on a wholesaler who hasn't done a deal yet. Work with them and do whatever you can to help them out. If you're helping them out, they should come to you once they do get a deal.

3. *Real Estate Agents*

I know it's getting repetitive talking about Real Estate Agents, but they're so important to what you do! If you have a good one, do everything you can to take care of them. I've had agents bring me many deals, but it was because we had built a relationship. If they don't know who I am or what I'm looking for, then they can't ever bring me a deal. You have to constantly be networking and creating more relationships. I go to lunch or meet for coffee with agents every week. My odds of getting a deal from an agent are significantly higher after meeting with them in person. Once you've built up relationships with agents, they'll be able to send you deals in a number of ways:

1. *Pocket Listings*

These would be homes that aren't on the market but the agent knows of a potential opportunity. It could be a friend, family member, or a client of the agent. Pocket Listings are great because there isn't any competition for them yet. Once a property hits the MLS, anyone in the world with the internet knows about it. You have a huge advantage negotiating with the seller before that happens.

An agent would bring you this deal, because you've built a relationship with them and they know you can close fast. They also might want to represent both parties in the transaction and get double the commission. That's fine! Don't be offended or think they're greedy. If the numbers work for you, then buy the home. If you do that deal, the agent is going to bring you the next one as well.

2. *MLS Deals*

This goes back to all the different MLS searches we talked about. There are a lot of deals on the MLS, you just need to find them. Even with all the searches we set up, some will still fall through the cracks. If you have multiple agents looking on the MLS for you, then you'll have a better chance of finding more of them. Agents have relationships with other agents, so they might have more insight on a property.

For this method to work, you need to make sure you're trustworthy. If an agent brings you a property and you want to make an offer, you had better let them represent you. I let other agents know I'm an agent, but I let them represent me if they find a deal. Because of that, trust has been built between us. I could easily take every lead someone sends me and make an offer on it myself so I can get the commission. That isn't the right way to treat people or run a business. By doing that, you would never get a deal sent from that agent again. Your reputation would also be ruined, so don't be greedy. If someone finds you a deal, let them get paid.

4. *Door Knocking*

This is a simple way to get Free Leads. Door Knocking is exactly how it sounds. You knock on doors and see if you can make a deal! You can walk a whole block of homes and knock as many doors as possible. You could do forms of targeted door knocking as well. If you know someone is in foreclosure or has some other type of problem, go and knock on their door! The most effective way of talking to someone is in person.

I know it's not easy to go knock on a stranger's door. It can be quite frightening. You will get a lot of people who tell you to get off their property. If you can get over that fear, it can make you a lot of money! I don't knock on many doors, but when I do, it's always targeted knocking. I know the seller is motivated and I want to meet face to face. I want the chance to prove to them that I can solve their problem. I know people who have success knocking on every door on the block. There is no right way to do it. The key is to take action and do something!

5. *Driving for Dollars*

To do this, drive around neighborhoods and look for beat up properties. Look for missing shingles, overgrown lawns, old exterior paint, busted garages, and beat up cars in the driveway. Most people drive for dollars in their cars but you could make it a workout! Take a run or bike ride around the block you're looking in. I bought an electric scooter specifically to ride around neighborhoods. I don't get a workout doing it, but I have a lot of fun zipping around on it. I liked doing it so much that I bought my wife a scooter so we could look at properties together. She likes to ride around and look at nice properties. I like looking at the beat-up ones. Either way, we get to spend time together, have fun, and potentially make money!

Besides having fun, why would we drive for dollars? Sellers who can't take care of their home usually have a problem. When there is a problem, there is potential for a deal.

Once you get a list of all of these beat-up homes, you need to contact them. The cheapest way is to knock on their door! It's the most straightforward, and since you're at the home when you see it, you might as well knock. If you want to do a high volume, then you can get your list of homes and send the owners letters saying you'd like to buy their home. We'll go over this strategy more in the next chapter.

6. *Social Media*

The last method of finding Free Leads is through social media. I've mentioned how important social media is numerous times. I'm repeating it again because it's that important! Plus, you don't learn anything without practice and repetition, so I'm going to keep repeating it! If you're actively showing your real estate journey on social media, deals will find you. I've gotten so many deals through social media and they never have cost me a dime. I've had many Realtors and wholesalers find me on social media and bring me deals. I've also had friends and family members refer me to someone who needed to sell their home.

None of that can happen unless people know you're an active real estate investor. Start building up your social media profile and let people know what you're doing. Deals will find you!

CHAPTER 8:

Paid Leads

Starting out I didn't have the money to pay for leads. I had to figure out how I could find deals freely, so I had enough money to buy them. All the methods in the previous chapter can get you started if you're low on cash. If you have money and you want to increase the amount of leads coming in, these next methods will be great for you. Make sure you use them in addition to the Free Leads methods.

1. *Website and SEO*

This is a costly way to get leads, but it is the best way to build a brand and credibility. You start by creating a website. The website will let people know that your company buys homes in your local area. If you don't know what it should look like, search terms like "we buy houses" and "cash offer for home." See what websites pop up and you'll get an idea of what your website should look like.

Once you create a website, you can choose if you want to do SEO (search engine optimization) on it. This isn't cheap if you do it right. Basically you'll be paying someone to get your website ranked high on Google searches. When someone is searching to get an offer on their home, your website will pop up. Plan to spend thousands a month if you want to get on the first page of Google.

Whether you choose to do SEO or not is up to you. But you should definitely spend the money to create a website. That alone will lead to more deals because it brings credibility. It makes a huge difference when your offer comes from a professional email instead of a Gmail address. Sellers, agents, and wholesalers take notice of that. You should have a signature at the bottom of the email that leads to your website and has an office address. If you don't have an office, you can pay $50 a month to have a virtual office. They give you an address and place to have your mail sent to. This is what I did starting out so that I could have a business address.

I've seen many people have success without a website. They could have even greater success if they did have a website. Creating a website is a relatively low cost these days. You can have someone do it on a website like Fiverr.com for very little. If it gets you just one more deal, then it was well worth it.

2. *Google and Social Media Ads*

Back in the day, Google AdWords was the only way to buy ads. Today we have so many different social media ads we can do. This includes Facebook, Instagram, Twitter, YouTube, and so on. How you choose to utilize them is up to you. To effectively do this, you need to have a website that you can link the ad to. Don't do this until you have a website. Once you have a good website, then spend the money and see if you can drive traffic to it.

3. *Direct Mail*

When I first started out, most people were recommending Direct Mail as the best source of leads. It's still very popular today, but it's very competitive. There are websites now that make Direct Mail very easy to do. They let you pick the list of people you want to mail to. Then you pick one of their templates that you want to use for the letter or postcard. Lastly, you choose when to have them sent out.

It's simple, but it can get costly. One piece of mail can cost you $1 and you need to send at least 1,000 a month to be effective. Most people fail at Direct Mail because of two reasons. They either send less than a thousand, or they send 1,000+ but quit after a month because it didn't produce a deal.

The Direct Mail response rate is usually 1% to 3%. So if you send 1,000 pieces out, then you should get 10 to 30 people who call you. That's not a lot of people to make a deal with. So you have to be willing to spend at least $1,000 for six straight months regardless of the results. Once you have six months of leads built up, then you can really see the results. If you can't make that commitment, then don't bother doing Direct Mail. There will be other methods that will be more effective for you.

4. *Cold Call*

This is one of my favorite Paid Leads. I currently have a call center in my office, and my team calls homeowners all day. But you don't need to pay to have a call center. You can make the calls yourself starting out. All you need to do is get a list of phone numbers for sellers and start making calls! There are websites that will provide different lists of sellers. I like this method, because if we can get a motivated seller on the phone, there's a good chance we can make a deal.

The issue with this method is the training required. Callers must be trained on how to correctly respond to sellers. They must be able to handle rejection. Sellers are going to yell and curse them out. Remember, 99% of the people we call won't end up making a deal with us. You must make a lot of calls in order to do a lot of deals.

5. *Bandit Signs*

We talked about Bandit Signs as a way to find wholesalers. They can also be a way to find deals if you're the one putting them out. All you need to do is get a bunch of signs made. A good size for a sign is 18 by 24 inches. What you put on it is up to you. I've seen many different variations of the signs.

There are three things to make sure of before putting up Bandit Signs:

1. Make sure it's legal in your city! Some cities don't allow them, so make sure you're not breaking the law.

2. Put them in areas where cars stop. I've seen them on freeways or in the middle of main streets. I've wanted to write the numbers down, but I never got a chance because I was driving by them! Make sure they're at stop signs or stop lights.

3. Hang them high up. If they're low, people will rip them off or vandalize them. Bring a ladder and put them up high enough so that no one can mess with them.

6. *Billboards*

I've tried all the methods above, but I haven't tried Billboards. I see them everywhere and I know a lot of big companies use them, so they must work. I don't know if they'll work for everyone. If you get one, make sure you have a website! It does you no good if they like your Billboard but can't find you online.

Paid Leads Conclusion

There are many ways to get Paid Leads. Everyone's market is different; methods that are great for me might not work for you. The only way to find out is by testing and seeing what produces the best results. Give each method enough time to see how well it performs. If you only do it for a month, then you're not getting enough data to see if it works or not.

Most successful flippers use a combination of these methods. Find the best ones and go all in on those. You don't need to do each one if you have a couple that are producing far above the rest.

CHAPTER 9:

Making Offers

Up to this point we've learned how to create lead sources and evaluate deals. As every lead comes in, we're calculating our Max Offer from Chapter 6. Your Max Offer will usually be below the seller's asking price. I've bought plenty of properties under my Max Offer, but that was because we negotiated. Don't be discouraged that you're always below what they are asking for the property. Negotiating is the key to making deals happen. Here are the rules for making offers:

1. **You should be embarrassed by your offer.** If you're not embarrassed by your offer, then you offered too much. You are going to get yelled at by sellers. Agents will tell you you're crazy. All that means is you're making the right type of offers. Don't let anyone discourage you as you make offers. There will be plenty of people who will try. Just ignore them.

2. **Make the offer no matter how far off you are.** If you've already evaluated a deal and done the work, you might as well make the offer. Let's say a seller wants $200,000 and your *Max Offer* is $140,000. Offer $130,000 and see what happens. They'll probably tell you to take a hike, but there is a chance they want to negotiate. If they do, then you still have some room to come up to $140,000. This makes it look like you're giving the seller something

and compromising. I've made many offers where the deal seemed unlikely, but ended up working out.

3. **Make lots of offers daily.** We've established that the majority of your offers will not get accepted. You need to make a lot of them in order to get deals. Make offers on every deal you evaluate. I make an offer on a home every day.

4. **You don't need to see the home in person to make offers.** As we talked about in the Repair Costs section, you can come up with a pretty good repair budget just by using P/Sq Ft. If there are pictures, you should be able to tell if it's going to be $10 or $20 per square foot for Repair Costs. I make all my offers based on pictures. If one gets accepted, then I will check it out in person and verify. If it's worse than in the pictures, then you can renegotiate or cancel during your due diligence period (more on that in the next chapter).

5. **Be quick with your offers.** A lot of times the key to getting a deal is being fast! I have a wholesaler who blasts out their deals to everyone and they take the first person who says yes. I've trained myself to be able to look at the address and pictures and say yes within 30 seconds. That's how quickly their deals go. That's an extreme example.

   A normal example would be deals on the MLS. I get a lot of those because I'm the first one to make an offer that day. I try to get the seller to negotiate with me before all the other offers come in. People who procrastinate or don't see the deal until the next day have already missed out.

Those are the rules for making offers. If you follow them, you should have some success getting them accepted. If you're making a lot of offers, it gets time consuming for you and your Realtor to write up that many offers. That's why I don't do that. I only write up an offer if I know I'm close to making a deal. I have two different strategies for how I present offers. One is for MLS deals and the other is for direct-to-seller deals.

MLS Deals

1. **Text.** Almost all real estate agents text now, so this is an easy way to reach them. I text them some form of this:

    Hey (name),

    I'd like to make a cash offer of (offer price) on the property at (address). We can close in less than 2 weeks and buy it as is. Would this get the deal done?

    Ryan Pineda

    (my website)

    It's quick and to the point. I spend one minute to write up that offer instead of 15 minutes to do the actual contract. The last question gives them something to respond to and create some engagement. They might say, "No that's too low, the seller wouldn't take that, but (new price) would get it done."

    I include my website under my name. My website is my resume and it shows homes I've bought and sold. Sometimes, I'll include a link to my Facebook profile so they can put a face to a name. My Facebook profile shows everything I'm doing in real estate and it builds more credibility. The more I can prove to the agent that I will close the deal, the more likely I am to get it.

2. **Email.** This is very similar to the text. I prefer text because agents usually respond faster. If they don't respond to the text, I will send this email:

    Subject: (Property Address) CASH OFFER

    Hey (name),

I'd like to make a cash offer of (offer price) on the property at (address). We can close in less than 2 weeks and buy it as is. Would this get the deal done?

Ryan Pineda

(Email Signature)

So it's the same exact message. The only difference is the subject line and the email signature. I want "CASH OFFER" to stand out in the subject line. They won't be able to miss it when they're going through emails.

You should have a professional email signature. Mine includes a headshot, business title, business address, business website, and my personal Facebook and Instagram. I want to build as much credibility as possible when I submit an offer. If you don't have any of those things yet, start creating them now!

Email and text allow you to keep a record of all the offers you've submitted. I make a lot of offers that don't get accepted, so I forget about them. Sometimes, the properties I offer on come back on the market. When I go to make an offer on them, I can see that I've offered before. Now I can tell the agent that I've been watching the property and I still want to buy it. This gives me an advantage over other offers now.

3. **Phone call.** This is my last resort if I can't get ahold of them with a text or email. I'm not big on making phone calls because they take more time and I can't track them as well. If a property is back on the market, I can't remember what the agent and I had talked about. With email and text, I can look back at what we discussed.

   The other downside to phone calls is I can't include my website or social media. In a phone call, they can't look me up to see if I'm credible. So make sure after a phone call, you text all your information so they can look you up afterwards.

Making the phone call is inevitable. I don't mind talking on the phone. I just want it to be after we've texted or emailed and we're close on a deal.

Those are the ways to make offers quickly. If they agree to the terms, then you can write the actual contract.

When you contact these agents, you have a better chance to get the deal if you let the listing agent represent you. I have done that when I felt like that was the only way to get the deal. But don't do that if another agent brought you the deal. Always make your offer through the agent who found it. Don't go around them and let the listing agent represent you because you want a better deal. That isn't the proper way to do business and if you do that, your investing career won't last very long.

Always treat people the right way, especially if they're bringing you a deal. If you found the property, you can mention in the text or email, "I would like you to write up the offer for me." This will get the listing agent excited to make a deal work so they can make double the commission. You'd be amazed how much more responsive they get upon hearing that.

Direct to Seller Deals

It's different when you're negotiating with a seller as opposed to an agent. A lot of times, sellers don't have an asking price. They may not have a clue what the property is worth. Talking about the price isn't the right approach. This is the correct approach:

Figure out what their problem is and find a way to solve it.

In order to solve a problem, you need to spend time talking and getting to know them. Building rapport is so important when dealing directly with sellers. If you ask the right questions and listen, then you will figure out how to get the deal done. If you're strictly worried about how cheap you can get the property for, you will struggle to make a deal. Here are some questions I use to figure out the seller's problem.

1. **Why do you need to sell the house?** This question actually serves two purposes. The first is to make sure they're actually motivated to sell. That's why we say, "Why do you *need* to sell?" If they say, "I don't *need* to sell, but I'd like to hear an offer," then there probably isn't a deal there. These people are usually wasting time or they want a lot more than you'll be able to pay.

The other purpose of this question is to find out the actual reason for wanting to sell. Common reasons I've heard are:

I need to sell because I'm moving to a new state.

If this is the case, then we need a few follow-up questions answered:

*   When do they need to move?
*   Do they need help moving?
*   Do they know where they're going to live?
*   How much money do they need to move?

If you can solve all those problems for them, they'll be willing to work with you.

I lost my job and can't make the mortgage payments anymore.

In this situation we need a few more questions answered:

*   How many payments have they missed?
*   Has there been a notice of sale or default?
*   How much do they owe on the mortgage?

The more you understand about the missing payments, the better you can help them get out of the problem.

I have a bad tenant and can't get rid of them.

You should then ask:

- Has the tenant wrecked the place?

- How long is their lease?

- How many rent payments behind are they?

You need to know what you're up against in order to get the tenant out.

All these follow up questions allow you to build rapport to figure out the problem. If you solve the problem, then the seller will do the deal with you. It's not always about money and price.

2. **How much money do you need to walk away with?** This one is important, because it gets them less focused on price and more focused on the result. Let's say they wanted $200,000 for the home. You then ask, "How much do you need to walk away with?" They tell you $50,000. From there you can ask, "Do you know how much you owe on the home?" They answer $133,000. Now you can tell them that if they owe $133,000 and need to walk away with $50,000, then $183,000 would get them what they want. Once you break it down like that, how can they say no? You'd be surprised how many sellers don't know how much they actually need.

3. **Is that the best you can do?** This is a question for sellers who are only focused on price. If they don't want to tell you their problem or don't have a ***need*** to sell, then ask them if their price is the best they can do. Sometimes, they will negotiate against themselves before you ever make an offer!

Always ask as many questions as you can before you actually make an offer. It will give you more information on how to make the best offer possible. It also helps build rapport with the seller and lets them know you want to create a deal that benefits both parties. By asking a lot of questions, you're making it about the seller and allowing them to speak. Most people like to talk more than they like to listen. I've done many deals where I barely spoke, but I listened to the seller vent for 30 minutes. Being a good listener will help you negotiate better and get you more deals!

Offer Details

Now that we've gone over negotiating techniques and how to make offers, we need to go over what's actually in the offer. Contracts vary state by state. I use a standard Realtor contract for my MLS deals. For my direct to seller deals, I use a three-page contract I created. The smaller contract is easier to understand and it makes the seller feel more comfortable. You can get the contract I use for free at FlipYourFutureBook.com/contract

Both contracts contain the same basic elements:

Purchase Price. How much we're buying the house for.

Close Date. What day the house is closing.

Earnest Money Deposit (EMD). The deposit you put on the house to show that you're going to purchase. This goes to the Title Company and is applied towards your Purchase Price. You're at risk of losing this money if you don't close on the property, and this proves to the seller that you are a motivated buyer.

Due Diligence Period. The time to get your Contractor bids and inspections done. If everything comes back good, then you can proceed with the deal. If it's more work than you anticipated, then you need to renegotiate or back out of the deal. If you don't back out during your Due Diligence period, you could lose your EMD.

Loan Contingency. The time you have to get your loan approved. If your loan gets denied during the contingency period, then you can back out and get your EMD back.

Closing Costs. All the fees for the Title Company and the Transfer Taxes. It needs to be stated which parties are responsible for which fees.

There are a lot more terms in contracts, but those are the most important ones. Purchase Price is what we've been focused on throughout the book, but if you use these other terms correctly, it can separate you from an offer with the same Purchase Price.

Here are some ways I use those terms to make my offer better. I don't recommend these strategies for beginners because they are riskier. If you have some experience, they could separate you from another offer and make you a lot of money:

1. **One-day Due Diligence Period**. The standard Due Diligence Period is 7 to 10 days. Doing only one day is much riskier, but it tells them you're willing to do inspections the same day and get the deal done quickly. It also shows them that after one day, you're willing to risk losing your EMD because you're confident in the deal.

2. **Bigger EMD than they're asking for.** Just like the One-day Due Diligence, you're putting your EMD at risk. As long as you know you're going to buy the property, it will make your offer look stronger. The Purchase Price doesn't change, but it shows the Seller you're willing to do more than necessary to get the deal done.

3. **No Loan Contingency.** I've got different financing sources and my own cash, so I'm not ever worried about whether a loan will close or not. If you're confident in your financing, you can do this as well.

4. **Pay all the closing costs.** When negotiating directly with sellers, you should pay all the closing costs. It helps them know exactly how much they're netting. It also gives you leverage to get the price you want because you're doing them a favor by covering all the closing costs.

5. **Close Date in one week.** As we discussed before, most loans take 30 to 45 days to close and a cash deal usually takes 14 days. By letting them know you can close in one week or less, it gives you a huge advantage

with sellers. You can let them know it's possible to even close before one week depending on how quick the Title Company works. This is probably the biggest thing that will get you more deals if you're able to do it.

These are more advanced strategies to get more deals. Don't try and do them on your first few deals.

Let's assume now that you've negotiated and made offers, you were able to get one accepted! We need to go over what happens next, which is the escrow process:

1. **Deposit your EMD.** Usually you have 24 to 48 hours to deposit.

2. **Get your inspections and contractor bids.** Once the offer is accepted, your due diligence period begins. You need to get your inspections and bids done before your due diligence ends.

3. **Work on your loan.** You now have until your close date to finalize your loan. You should have sent your lender all the required paperwork the day the offer was accepted. If you've got a 14-day close, every day counts, so don't waste time.

4. **Final Walkthrough.** When your loan has been approved, you walk through the property one more time to make sure it's in the same condition as when you did your inspections. I once heard from an investor that they did a walk through on the day they were supposed to close and found out the house had burnt down. The seller didn't say anything about it! So make sure you always do your walk through before you close.

5. **Close on the house.** When the final walkthrough goes well, wire your remaining down payment and the loan funds. After that, the Title Company gets everything and records the sale. Now you own the property!

CHAPTER 10:

Construction Time

So up to this point you've completed half the battle. You found a deal and purchased it. Now you need to rehab and sell it. Let's go over the steps in the construction process.

1. *What work to do?*

   You need to decide what repairs you want to make to the home. This includes what color schemes and finishes to use. I can't tell you what you should do, because it's all going to depend on your market and your style. You wouldn't put the same type of finishes in a $500,000 home as you would in a $150,000 home. Also, $200,000 homes in different areas will require different finishes. So how do you decide what to do? **Copy the comps!**

   Remember how we went over ARV and searched for similar homes? Look up those homes and see what color schemes, styles, and finishes they used. Then do the exact same thing as them! It already sold for what you want yours to sell for, so why mess with it? When I first started out, I tried all types of random color schemes and styles. Some worked well and others didn't. Then one day I realized that all the more experienced flippers' homes looked similar. I decided to make mine look like theirs, and guess what happened? My homes started selling much faster!

Now I use the same color scheme in the majority of my homes, because it sells. It's also one less decision I have to worry about. If I had to decide a new color scheme on every home, it would be a lot of work. Don't be afraid to do what the competition is doing. I don't even like the colors and style I use! I wouldn't put those finishes in my own home. Buyers like it though, so that's all that matters!

2. *Choose Your Contractor*

You should have your bids during the due diligence process. I recommend that you always get three contractor bids on every property. It helps keep your contractors in check and insures that you get the best price. Also it gets you three different eyes on the property. One of them might miss a big problem that the other one sees. One might have a really good idea to add a bedroom or open up the floor plan. You will get a better plan and a better price by getting more bids.

Once you get your bids, you need to compare them and see what they're covering. Just because you talked about it at the property, doesn't mean it's in the actual bid. You need to make sure it's on paper so there is no confusion later on. Take into account how long it took them to get you the bid. It's a good thing if they get it to you quickly. If they're late in getting it to you, then they might be late on the job.

It's not always about who's the cheapest. How quickly they can do the job plays a role. We talked earlier about the Money Costs and the Holding Costs. If one guy is going to take an extra month to do the work, then it adds up! Make sure you have their time frame on the bid. If two contractors tell you it will take 8 weeks to do and the other one only says 4 weeks, realize it's probably really going to take 8 weeks. Many contractors will say they can do it faster just to get the job.

Lastly, realize the contractor is trying to get a job. They may tell you all the things you want to hear. You need to always to be on guard with what you believe. I have a lot of good contractors, but I can tell when they stretch the truth in order to get a job. It might be on time frame or staying on budget. So keep your guard up!

3. *Payments*

Contractors will try to get you to pay a lot of money up front. Don't give them that much. I still don't do it even if they've done other jobs for me. I don't like to have a contractor get ahead of me. What that means is, if I were to fire them today, would it cost me more to finish the project with another contractor? If the answer is yes, then they were ahead of me. If they're ahead, then there is always the possibility that they might walk away or skip town. If they're behind you, then they'll want to keep working so they can get what they're owed.

Initially, you will be behind because you need to give them some start-up money. They need to get materials and pay their subcontractors. After the initial payment, make sure they're doing good work. Don't give them another payment until they've done more work than what that first initial payment covered. The goal is to get ahead of them as soon as you can. Sometimes it takes longer because they need to pay for big-ticket material items. That's OK as long as they're working and doing a good job.

Be safe when paying them. Come up with a payment plan before the job starts. On a $20,000 job, you might pay them $2,000 to get started. After that, you pay four payments of $4,500. It protects you and gives them enough money to keep the job going. Some contractors need to be paid weekly. That's fine, but make sure you break the payments up properly. If you see they're behind schedule, you need to make sure they don't get paid until they get back on schedule.

You have to check on the property in order to know if they're on schedule. All of my properties are checked once or twice a week. This is to make sure jobs are moving, and it keeps contractors on their toes. If you're never at the job site and they ask for money, then how can you know if they deserve it? You or someone needs to be there to confirm the work being done. That person should be taking pictures every time they're there. It helps to keep a record and protect you from any disagreements. It will be good content for social media. You can show progress pictures and videos of you walking through a job site. People like seeing that stuff!

4. *Change Orders*

This is the biggest cause of problems during a renovation. Change orders are any extra costs that the bid didn't cover. During renovations it's common for things to pop up as extra costs. Maybe they open up a wall and they find that all the plumbing needs to be replaced. Perhaps they found mold when they pulled the cabinets out. There are a lot of justifiable change orders that happen. You must let your contractor know that you need to approve all of them before they do them. One time a contractor billed me $5,000 in change orders on the final payment. I never approved any extra things nor did he tell me about them during the renovation. Be clear from the beginning that you're not paying any change orders unless they're approved.

Some contractors will give you a low bid knowing that they'll make it up in change orders on the back end. You need to be aware of that throughout the process. Don't let them tell you something is a change order when it's already in the bid. If they try to do unjustified change orders at the end, don't use them again. Unfortunately, there's no way to tell if you're dealing with that type of contractor until you use them.

5. *Walk Through*

Once the job is complete, you do a final walk through. You walk through and check the quality of the work and make sure they didn't miss anything. Bring a blue roll of paint tape so that you can mark all the spots that need to be touched up. The biggest thing you'll find usually are paint touch ups. Put the tape on all the spots that need it. Check all the cabinets and drawers to make sure they slide and close properly. Turn on all the lights to see if any don't work. Test the showers, faucets, and toilets to see if there are any leaks. Walk around the house and inspect the floors. Make sure all the tiles and laminate aren't loose. Test the AC to make sure it's running properly. Look at the bid and make sure everything on there was done. If you find something wrong with the house that wasn't on the bid, get an estimate to repair it.

Contractor Conclusion

There are a lot of good contractors and a lot of bad ones. If you find a good, trustworthy, and fairly priced contractor, make sure you take care of them. Keep them busy so that they don't leave you for another investor. High-quality contractors who are priced well are not easy to find! You can do everything to find contractors, but you don't know how good they are until you try them out. That's the scary part! As long as you're safe with your payments, you should be fine.

If a contractor isn't working out, do not be afraid to fire them. I've been known for being really soft on my guys. I have a hard time firing people! Sometimes you have to do it, though. If they're not doing good work or they're taking too long, then you need to address it. Let them know your concerns and remind them of your expectations. Let them know that they're on notice and you're going to reevaluate the progress in a week. If you're not seeing progress a week later, then get rid of them.

Finally, understand that contractors are going to come and go. Maybe your personalities don't mesh well. Perhaps your expectations are too high for what they can achieve. There will be a higher turnover of contractors more than anyone else on your Dream Team. Don't be discouraged by it. Continue to look for more even if you don't need them yet. I found some of my best contractors months before I ever had the opportunity to use them. Once I tried them out, I realized how great they were! Look for contractors more than any other member of your Dream Team!

CHAPTER 11:

The Sale

We've reached the final step in the Flipping Process! It took a lot of work to get to this point. Now that the renovation is done, it's time to get the property on the market! Here are the steps.

1. *Pictures*

There is one rule for this step: **Hire a professional**. Bad or even average pictures will cost you thousands of dollars! People see homes based on the pictures. A good photographer is worth the $100 to $300 they charge. I don't care if you have a nice camera or the newest iPhone. Hire a professional, it's non-negotiable.

2. *Hire Realtor*

Once you have pictures, it's time to choose a Realtor! You should have a couple on your Dream Team. Let them see the property and give you their take on the value. Find out what type of commission they would want. Don't always go with the cheapest one. You want the one who will net you the most money. If they're able to get you a higher price because they're a better negotiator or marketer, then they're worth a bigger commission. Also, don't always go with the one who thinks it's worth the highest price. They might be telling you what you want to hear just so they can get the listing. It could cost you thousands in holding costs by pricing it too high and having it sit. Choose the Realtor you feel the most comfortable with and who has your best interests in mind.

3. *Decide on List Price*

As you decide on the list price it's good to get multiple opinions. It's the same process as when you get bids with contractors. You want to know why they think their price is correct. Maybe they see something the other Realtors don't see. Ask other people in your network as well. One time, I was going to list a property for $200,000 based on my evaluation. I asked one of my mentors his opinion and he told me to list at $220,000. I took his advice and in the first week I got a full price offer at $220,000! My mentor made me an extra $20,000 just with one piece of advice! One piece of advice can have a huge impact on your income. Always be looking for multiple opinions.

When I decide on list price, this is what I'm looking at in order of importance:

Sold Properties. We calculated ARV before we bought the home. Now it needs to be calculated again. The comps will be different from the time you first evaluated the deal. Run the comps again and see if the numbers have changed.

Active Properties. You need to know what similar homes are on the market right now. If there are no other move-in-ready homes, then you control the market. You can price it higher than the comps and see if someone will pay for it.

If there are a lot of comparable homes on the market, then you can't use that strategy. You should be priced the same or below those homes. If you're above them, then buyers will see the cheaper ones instead. So always know what you're competing against.

Contingent Sales. These properties have already accepted offers. They won't affect you too much, but be aware of them. If one is going to sell for a higher price than the rest of the comps, you might want to match their price. If there are a lot of active properties and the contingent sale is significantly lower, then you might want to be priced the same as the contingent sale.

Take all these factors into account. The Sold Properties and Active Properties are going to help determine your List Price the most. Listen to your Realtors and network. My last listing tip is to always shoot high on a list price and come down later. You can change your price the next week if it didn't get any showings. If you price too low from the beginning, you might end up selling yourself short of potential profits.

4. *On Market*

Once you pick your List Price, it's time to put the property on the market and see what happens. It is best to put the property on the market Thursday or Friday. That makes it a new listing for the weekend. The weekend is where a lot of buyers are seeing homes. It's not mandatory to list on those days, though. If the property is ready on Monday, go ahead and list it. Remember, the interest on the loan is adding up daily!

Once it's listed, there are a couple different scenarios that can play out. Here are the best, normal, and worst cases.

Best Case

You get multiple offers on the property and you have to decide how to proceed. This is a great problem to have. You can do three things in this scenario.

Accept the best offer. The best offer isn't always the highest purchase price. You might get a cash offer from someone who can close quickly with no issues. I always try to work with cash if I can.

Counter the best offer. Maybe the best offer has some terms you don't like. It could be the price, close date, due diligence length, and so on. Counter with the terms you're willing to sell the property for.

Request Highest and Best. You inform all the offers that there are multiple offers and you're requesting their Highest and Best Offers. Usually you give them 24 to 48 hours to change their offer if they would like.

I've used all these strategies before. They need to be used on a case-by-case basis. Accepting the best offer would be good if it's way above the rest. Asking for Highest and Best would be good if you have a lot of similar offers. Countering the best offer would be good if you have a cash offer but you need to change a term. Every situation is different, and you need to consult with your Realtor on what strategy is best for the property.

If you get one offer in the first week on the market, that is a best-case scenario as well. You can't use highest and best, but you still have a lot of power. If it's a great offer, then you can accept it. If it's not what you want, then go ahead and counter it. You hold the power, since it hasn't been on the market long.

Normal Case

The normal case would be the property is on the market for three to four weeks before getting an offer. You don't have the power that you have in the Best Case situation, but you're not giving the property away, either. Maybe you're not going to get all the terms you wanted, but you're going to meet in the middle somewhere. Both sides want to make a deal and need to come to a compromise. So find a way to make a deal happen that works for everyone!

Worst Case

If your property hasn't gotten an offer for a month that it's been on the market, then you need to figure out the problem. It could be a number of things:

Are you overpriced? Check the Active Properties and see what your competition is. If there is a lot, then you're probably overpriced.

Is there something wrong with the house? Look at your house and see what it looks like compared to the comps. Maybe your floor plan sucks. Perhaps you have a noisy main street behind you. You might have a neighbor scaring everyone away. I've seen all types of things. You need to see what the problem is and fix it.

Is the listing correct? I've had listings where the agent clicked a box that didn't allow the home to show up on websites like Zillow. That's a killer, since most people are browsing on there! I've also had listings where the description was bad or there was an error in one of the details. Check and make sure there is nothing going on there.

Once you solve the problem, then the property should get more offers. You might have a mix of all three things if it's really bad! From my experience, it's typically the price that is the issue. If a property has been on the market for over a month, I drop the price every week. The first price drop can be significant, so that it's priced correctly with the comps. The next price drops can be $100 to $500. It doesn't seem like that would do anything, but it actually refreshes the listing. People on auto searches will have it pop up as a price drop. It's a trick you can use to get your property new action without really dropping the price.

5. *Accepting an Offer*

We talked about how to negotiate and choose the best offer in the previous step. Choosing the best offer isn't always about the highest price. You may want to take the cash offer even if it's less, so you get the quick close. There are other variables to think about when choosing an offer.

Closing Costs. Typically, closing costs are 2% to 3% of the purchase price. This covers all the buyer's loan and title company fees. Buyers may ask the seller to pay for these costs. If they offer $200,000 for the property, but want $6,000 in closing costs, then their offer is really $194,000. This is why the highest offer may not be the best.

Lender. When a buyer sends you an offer, they will include a prequalification letter from their lender. The letter says what price, loan type, and down payment the buyer is approved for. Unfortunately, these letters aren't hard to get. Even though they say they're "prequalified," it's not always the case. Your Realtor should call the lender and verify what they've done with the buyer. They should have run their credit, gotten tax returns, and gotten bank statements. If they haven't, then the letter is worthless. You want to make sure you're accepting an offer from someone who is going to close on the property. There is nothing worse than being in escrow for 45 days and then finding out the buyer won't qualify for the loan. They've wasted valuable time and cost you money. Make sure the buyer is truly prequalified before accepting their offer.

Loan Type. Be aware of what type of loan the buyer is getting before accepting an offer. There are three main loan types:

Conventional Loan. This is usually a 5% to 20% down payment loan. The buyer will usually have good credit and more cash than the other types of loans.

FHA Loan. This is a government-based loan with a 3.5% minimum down payment. The buyer's credit doesn't have to be as good for this loan. The buyer may also be gifted their down payment. Typically, buyers who use this loan don't have a lot of cash to put down.

VA Loan. This is a government-based loan only for people who have served in the military. The cool part about this loan is the buyer can put a 0% down payment. Sometimes these buyers don't have any cash. Other times they do, but they want to take advantage of the 0% down payment. I prefer accepting offers with this loan because it's nice to sell a home to a veteran and appraisals usually come in higher. If an appraiser comes in with a value less than the purchase price, they have to fill out more paperwork to justify the lower value. Appraisers are more inclined to give the value of the purchase price and not deal with the extra work.

6. *Home Inspection*

Once you've accepted an offer, the due diligence period begins. The buyer is going to hire a home inspector to find out all the problems with the home. No matter how nice a house is, the inspectors always find things wrong!

The inspector will spend a couple of hours at the house. They will create a report of all the things wrong and send it to the buyer. The buyer has to decide what they want to do next. They may elect to cancel the deal if the report scares them. If they want to stay in the deal, they'll send over a repair request form. You then have the option to repair everything they're asking for or send a counter with the repairs you're willing to make. Send the report to your contractor and see what should have been included in their original work. Your contractor should repair those items for free. You need to get a bid on the rest of the work they're requesting to be repaired. Once you come to an agreement with the buyer on what repairs are to be made, you can move on to the next step.

7. *Appraisal*

If a buyer is getting a loan, they also need to get an appraisal. An appraiser goes to the home and evaluates it. They then compare it to the comps and determine the value. The bank will use this value to base their loan from.

For example, if the buyer agrees to a $200,000 purchase price and the appraisal comes back at $190,000, then there is a problem. Someone will have to come up with the $10,000 difference. The first thing to do is file a rebuttal with the appraiser. This is a form you fill out with comps, repairs, and explanations for why you think it should have been $200,000. Submit it and see what happens. If they keep the appraisal at $190,000, then four different things can happen:

1. Buyer will pay the difference with their own cash.

2. Seller will drop the price to $190,000.

3. Buyer and seller will meet somewhere in between.

4. They can't agree and the buyer backs out of the deal.

Ideally, the buyer will pay the difference since they agreed on the price. But many times it's not possible. The buyer might only have enough cash for their down payment so they couldn't pay the difference if they wanted to. I had an appraisal come back $17,000 less and I had to drop the price by that much, because the buyer had no extra cash. That's a lot of lost profit!

8. *Loan Approval*

If you took a loan offer, all you can do is wait for the loan to be approved. If you took a cash offer, then this step is skipped along with the appraisal step. Cash offers are better, because there are fewer steps along the way. This means there are fewer potential things that can go wrong. Most sales will be loans, so learn to plan for that in the process.

9. *Final Walk Through*

Once the loan has been approved, the buyer will do their final walk through. They'll check to see if all the repairs have been made from the home inspection.

10. *Closing*

Both parties sign all the paperwork. The buyer wires the down payment and the lender funds the loan. The Title Company gets all the money and transfers the property. You have officially completed the flip! All the hard work up to this point has finally produced a profit. Go throw a party with your friends and family! Post your success on social media and let people know all the ups and downs that came with it. Sharing the experience will allow you to complete more flips just like this one.

CHAPTER 12:

Conclusion

Those are all the steps it takes to flip a house. It's not an easy process, but there is no reason you can't do it. The only question is: "Why do you want to do it?" Before I started, I wrote down a list of things I wanted and didn't want in my life.

I wanted:

- To spend as much time with family and friends as possible.
- To be able to travel whenever and wherever.
- Time to volunteer at my church.
- Financial freedom.
- To provide for my parents.

I didn't want:

- A job working for someone else.
- A limit on how much money I could make.
- Someone else in control of my schedule.

Write down your list and post it somewhere you can see everyday. This will help motivate you! Maybe you want to be able to buy your dream car. Perhaps you want to spend more time with your kids. Maybe you want to build a business and hire your friends. That wasn't one of my goals, but it ended up happening! My business has allowed me to hire my friends and family. It provided them a way out of jobs they hated! That has been one of the biggest blessings that house flipping has created for me.

Flipping houses can help you achieve the lifestyle you want. If you follow the steps in this book, you can make six figures your first year. You have all the tools to succeed. All that's left is to put in the work. It takes a lot of hard work and it doesn't happen overnight. So don't be discouraged if it is hard in the beginning.After you get your first deal, it gets easier and easier. The first deal is always the hardest! As your network and Dream Team grows, the deals will start pouring in! It's a constant game of growing and building relationships. You're going to make mistakes along the way, so embrace them and learn from them. Share the highs and the lows! They will help you grow your business even more.

The last thing I want you to do is find a mentor. I was very blessed to find one early in my journey. You need to do the same. Go to your local real estate meet-ups and join Facebook groups. Find the people who are doing a lot of flips and see if you can provide them some type of value. You may have to work for them for free. You might have to pay them. Either way, find one who will put the time into helping you grow.

In addition to having a local mentor, you should take the next steps in the *Flip Your Future System*. Go to FlipYourFutureBook.com and sign up for our email list. When you sign up, we will send you a free gift to help start your business. We also have different training programs in addition to this book. This includes Online Training Videos, Live Training Seminars, and Mentoring. These programs will amplify what you've learned in this book.

You have the game plan to succeed, and now it's time to take action! No amount of coaching and knowledge can replace action. I would be happy if you never read this book again, but took massive action instead! It's time to *Flip Your Future*. I look forward to hearing your success story!

10 Step Call to Action

1. Sign up for our email list at FlipYourFutureBook.com.

2. Announce your new journey on social media!

3. Choose a market you want to invest in.

4. Start networking and find your Dream Team.

5. Pick which Lead Sources you want to go after.

6. Make tons of offers on those leads.

7. Get your first offer accepted.

8. Flip your first house using everything you learned!

9. Celebrate and share your success!

10. Rinse and repeat to *Flip Your Future!*